THE GOOD THE BAD AND THE UGLY

THE GOOD THE BAD AND THE UGLY
The Story of Boxing

Frank Butler

Stanley Paul
London Melbourne Auckland Johannesburg

Copyright © Frank Butler 1986

All rights reserved

First published in 1986 by Stanley Paul & Co. Ltd, an imprint of Century Hutchinson Ltd, Brookmount House, 62–65 Chandos Place, Covent Garden, London WC2N 4NW

Century Hutchinson Australia (Pty) Ltd
16–22 Church Street, Hawthorn, Melbourne, Victoria 3122

Century Hutchinson New Zealand Ltd
32–34 View Road, PO Box 40–086, Glenfield, Auckland 10

Century Hutchinson South Africa (Pty) Ltd
PO Box 337, Bergvlei 2012, South Africa

Printed and bound in Great Britain by R. J. Acford, Chichester, Sussex

British Cataloguing in Publication Data
Butler, Frank
   The good the bad and the ugly : the story
   of boxing.
   1. Boxing — History
   I. Title
   796.8′3′09   GV1121

ISBN 0 09 1661102

Contents

Come Out Fighting — 1

Book One　The Good — 7

Super-Champions — 9
Sugar Ray Robinson — 12
Joe Louis — 17
Henry Armstrong — 22
Archie Moore — 25
Rocky Marciano — 28
Sugar Ray Leonard — 31
Marvin Hagler — 35
Roberto Duran — 39
Larry Holmes — 43
Alexis Arguello — 46
Don Curry — 48

The Best of British — 51
Jack Kid Berg — 53
Benny Lynch — 57
Len Harvey — 61
Tommy Farr — 65
Randolph Turpin — 70
Freddie Mills — 74
Howard Winstone — 78
Ken Buchanan — 83

Book Two The Bad 87
Monopoly 89
The Build-Up 98
Mismatches 105
Never Bet on Fights 109

Book Three The Ugly 113
Day of the Hoodlums 115
Exploitation 120
King Con 126
Violence Outside the Ring 130
The Drug Menace 138

Book Four The Agony 143
Three Tragic Worldbeaters 145
Skid Row 152
The Shame of a Brave Man 154
The Greek God 157
Lousy Requiem for a Heavyweight 159
His Own Executioner 162
Breakfast at Caesar's 165
Sweet and Sour 167
Nobbins for a Champ 170
Journey's End 172
The Mugging of a Legend 175

Book Five The Ecstasy 177
Something Special 179
Henry the One and Only 187
Warrior of Peace 192
TV's Golden Boy 196
The Tycoon 200

The Last Round 203

Index 209

Acknowledgements

For permission to reproduce copyright photographs, the author and publishers would like to thank Central Press, Associated Press, Sport & General Press Agency, Press Association, *News of the World*, All-Sport, *Daily Mail* and Sporting Pictures (UK).

COME OUT FIGHTING

Whether you regard boxing as a sweet science or a violent sport, it always has been, and always will be, involved in controversy. From its origins, which date back to the Greeks and Romans, the sport has been opposed by politicians and men of medicine. There remains a love–hate relationship between its friends and enemies within the House of Lords and the Commons and the British Medical Association. Some doctors in America and Australia back up their colleagues in Britain and want to see professional boxing banned, as it has been in Sweden (since 1969), Norway (since 1982) and all Communist countries. Ironically, since Sweden and Norway abolished boxing, a Swede and a Norwegian won the European heavyweight championship in succession, fighting in Denmark.

Despite medical and political hostility, boxing is flourishing worldwide, due mainly to television. The top performers collect far richer prizes than any other sporting kings. Jack Dempsey was the first sportsman to draw a million-dollar gate back in the twenties. Muhammad Ali raised the personal reward for one contest to $5 million in the seventies, while this record has been eclipsed by a middleweight, Marvin Hagler, in the eighties. World television enabled Ali and Hagler to earn more in one championship fight than Joe Louis received in a record twenty-five defences in a career lasting seventeen years.

Boxing will survive. Man is aggressive, and was born to fight or to be attracted by the spectacle of two other men in physical conflict. The risk of injury cannot be denied, for the aim of every competitor is to render his opponent unconscious. But there is an element of danger in many sports. Motor racing is dangerous because excessive speed can kill and every participant is out to reach a higher speed than his rivals. Horse racing has a long list of serious injuries among jump jockeys. Rugby, soccer and cricket all have their accidents.

Abolition seldom works. If boxing were prohibited in Britain, America or any country where it flourishes, the sport would be driven underground and control would cease to operate. Wherever prize fighting was illegal, contests were staged at secret venues in barns or on barges. Unscrupulous and sadistic gamblers who put on cock fights and dog fights moved in. Today there are unlicensed street fights staged without control or medical supervision. They are most distasteful.

Bob Arum, a highly successful Top Rank television boxing promoter in America with an obvious vested interest, scoffs at the notion of abolition. 'Who cares?' he asks. 'We'd purchase Top Rank barges and promote championships on rivers and the ocean.' Only a few would be present but millions would watch on television. Far better to have boxing controlled and under medical supervision. It is less of a hazard than allowing boys and young men to roam the streets and become sufficiently desperate to rob and mug. In a supervised gymnasium they can release suppressed violence on each other. Boxing gloves are less dangerous than flick knives or bicycle chains. Many fighters, including Sonny Liston, George Foreman, Floyd Patterson and Rocky Graziano, all of whom had a spell in a reform school, were helped by boxing and won world titles.

Prize fighting fascinated intellectuals such as William Hogarth and William Hazlitt. A Prime Minister, the Prince Regent and various dukes became patrons. After the brutal meeting between Tom Sayers, champion of England, and the American champion John C. Heenan at Farnborough, Hampshire, in 1860, a move was made in Parliament to have fighting universally banned throughout Britain. Lord Lovaine led the attack in the House while Lord Palmerston, the Prime Minister, defended fighting against what he described as an exaggerated and sensational assault. Though Lord Lovaine's motion of censure was carried, there was never a national ban, but many were shocked by the savagery of that fight, especially when Sayers, who never fought again, died of tuberculosis five years later when only thirty-nine.

The Queensberry Rules were introduced to take the brutality out of the sport which, through the years, has become safer with the introduction of very strict medical controls. I am convinced that boxing is better supervised in Britain than anywhere else in the world. There are many doctors and politicians who do not want to see boxing banned.

There have, of course, been abuses, as there have in horse racing, dog racing and every sport in which big money is involved. The British Boxing Board of Control has its critics, as have the Football Association, the Jockey Club, the Rugby Union, Lawn Tennis Association and other controlling bodies. I have often criticized the BBBC and, as a steward, I am willing to accept criticism. I have learned it is far easier to criticize than have to supply the solution.

In the summer of 1984 the BMA passed a motion at their annual general meeting in Manchester to campaign to influence public opinion to favour the eventual banning of boxing. Six months later the American Medical Association overwhelmingly adopted a similar resolution in Honolulu. The BMA claimed that since 1945 at least 340 boxers, amateurs and pros, had died throughout the world from injuries in the ring and hundreds more had been blinded or had their sight seriously impaired or suffered brain damage. BMA secretary John Harvard predicted that a ban in the United Kingdom might be achieved in five to ten years. I believe this to be wishful thinking. The BMA also pointed out that the Amateur Boxing Association and armed services had cooperated in giving evidence but regretted that the BBBC had declined. However, this was because the BBBC's suggestion that an independent inquiry should be held on the grounds that the BMA's report would of necessity be biased was ignored by the BMA. The World Medical Association and the Australian Medical Association had already issued anti-boxing reports following several fatalities in 1982. In response to these pressures the World Boxing Council, the European Boxing Union and the BBBC have ruled that championship contests must be reduced from

15 rounds to a maximum of 12. The World Boxing Association and the International Boxing Federation, however, retained 15-round championships. Some American states experimented with thumbless gloves without any obvious success. And though the BMA say that headguards are not protection against brain injury, all boxers in the 1984 Olympics at Los Angeles were compelled to wear them and ringside doctors were given the authority to override the referee if they believed a contest had been allowed to continue too long.

Not all doctors are anti-boxing by any means. Many enjoy watching it and several are happy to serve on the BBBC. Dr Adrian Whiteson, the Board's chief medical officer, is also a steward. He does not deny the risks but insists there are even greater risks of injuries in other sports. He maintains that Britain leads the world on safety, with the use of brain scans and intensive eye examinations. I can endorse the meticulous care Dr Whiteson and his committee take. While no brain damage was revealed in seventy cases, abnormalities were discovered after scans on David Pearce, the British heavyweight champion, and two American visitors to Britain in 1985. They were not allowed to box and Pearce's licence was withdrawn. Pearce still insists his abnormality was not caused through boxing and that he was born with it. In 1986 Dr Whiteson, Dr Oswald Ross and the Medical Committee drew up the most comprehensive set of safety plans ever attempted to protect boxers in their own interests.

Having said this, I repeat that boxing must be classed as a violent sport. To deny this or even to attempt to brush some of the risks under the carpet would only be to deceive oneself. Any boy or man who steps in the ring is at risk. Deaths have occurred after world championship bouts – witness Jimmy Doyle (*v.* Sugar Ray Robinson), Benny Paret (*v.* Emile Griffith), Davey Moore (*v.* Sugar Ramos) and Johnny Owen (*v.* Lupe Pintor). Robinson's left hook dropped Doyle and his head crashed to the canvas. He died after a brain operation. At the inquest the coroner asked Robinson, 'Did you intend to hurt Doyle?' The champion was frank. 'Mister, that's what my business is all about!' The magnificent Barry McGuigan from Ireland still mourns Young Ali, a little Nigerian who died after Barry knocked him out in 1982. McGuigan considered quitting, but a priest, a friend of the family, convinced him it was a complete accident, pointing out the risk every boxer takes.

The risks are not always in the ring. Ironically Victor Galindez, Argentina's former world light-heavyweight champion, retired from boxing in 1980 to become a racing driver. He was killed in his first race as he walked back to the pits after his machine had broken down. Had he died after one of his seventy fights the anti-boxing cry would have been loud.

Doctors who are against boxing refer to the 'punch-drunk' syndrome. Afflicted boxers are supposed to totter on their heels, slur their speech and suffer from a failing memory. This is splendid ammunition for reporters who find fiction stranger than truth and so much easier to write about. However, Jose Torres, former world light-heavyweight champion and now the respected chairman of New York State Athletic Commission, declared that he had never met a punch-drunk boxer. I can recall one or two old-timers who had fought too many twenty-round contests and seemed a little the worse for wear, but I have not seen a case for many years. Of course, some old boxers find their memories deteriorating, but if this is an accepted symptom of the syndrome I know an awful lot of punch-drunks who never wore a pair of boxing gloves in their lives.

While the anti-boxing lobby lists the number of casualties, boxing does not seem to have harmed some great champions who had many tough fights. Dempsey died a month before his eighty-eighth birthday, Tunney lived to eighty-one and Jess Willard died at ninety-six. Larry Gains lived to be eighty-two, Max Schmeling is a healthy octogenarian, and Jack Kid Berg and Jack Petersen are active and articulate in their seventies, as was Tommy Farr.

There have been some unscrupulous characters in boxing, especially in America, where the sport has a history of corruption. The notorious Frankie Carbo and his aid, Blinky Palermo, had an evil influence at world championship level in the forties and fifties. Champions were exploited and fights fixed until the federal government intervened. Even in 1984 the FBI investigated allegations of corruption and organized crime in boxing in New Jersey. The New Jersey state held an inquiry, but after two years and at a cost of $2 million to the taxpayers, there was no indictment of any promoter, manager or boxer, so the whole operation seemed a waste of time. Even so, there was an unsuccessful call to abolish boxing in New Jersey.

Boxing has boomed in that state with the arrival of Las Vegas-like gambling in hotels and casinos, and the call for the abolition of the sport has not completely gone away. One promoter and manager stand accused of having links with organized crime. On the other hand, the New Jersey commission claims it is in control and is confident boxing will survive there.

Meanwhile another new organization has appeared on the American scene – the Association of Boxing Commissioners – with the aim of improving safety and wisely campaigning to prevent promoters operating in any state which does not possess its own official commission. Happily, the new association has promised not to issue ratings or introduce any more titles to add to the already bizarre situation created by the World Boxing Council, the World Boxing Association and the International Boxing Federation, which between them have produced nearly fifty world champions where there once were only eight.

Everything is not perfect. In every barrel there is the danger of a rotten apple. It is the same with world boxing. I shall strive to deal with the good, the bad and the ugly aspects of the sport as fairly as possible.

BOOK ONE

THE GOOD

SUPER-CHAMPIONS

To attempt to rate the all-time greats would not only invite open conflict with readers but would be striving to achieve the impossible. We are all more easily impressed when very young and our heroes are inclined to grow in stature as we grow older. Comparing the past with the present proves nothing; it is only a matter of opinion and boxing writers, like racing tipsters, are frequently wrong. So I have selected a few champions who, for me, stood out from the rest. Only lack of space prevents me dealing with many more and I ask you to bear with me if you disagree with my choice and are disappointed if I have not done justice to your particular hero.

I became a precocious boxing fan on my seventh birthday when, as a special treat, my father took me to watch the debonair Frenchman Georges Carpentier, the scourge of British heavyweights, in training at Shoeburyness for his second fight with Joe Beckett, the British champion. Four years earlier he had flattened Beckett in 73 seconds before an exclusive gathering of 2000 dinner-jacketed fans who had paid twenty-five guineas to sit or five guineas to stand.

I was too young to form any judgement about the fight, but as Carpentier was extremely charming and bought me a box of chocolates he became my first boxing hero, especially as he knocked out Beckett in 48 seconds! I still treasure the autographed photo he gave me over sixty years ago. I was well and truly hooked to the sport by the time the two Dempsey–Tunney fights caused worldwide interest in 1926 and 1927, and I was thrilled to be able to collect their autographs when these outstanding heavyweights visited Britain. When, as an enthusiastic young reporter, I sailed for my first trip to America my first ports of call were on Dempsey and Tunney. Both were most helpful to me as a boxing rookie. I only saw Dempsey and Tunney in action on film but I have often wondered how Joe Louis or Muhammad Ali would have fared had it been possible for all these champions to have met at their peak.

The world knew really hard times in the thirties; unemployment without social security produced hungry fighters who became outstanding champions. I was privileged to see in action the likes of Max Baer, Young Stribling, Tommy Loughran, Bob Olin, Freddie Miller, Panama Al Brown, Henry Armstrong, Joe Louis, Sugar Ray Robinson, Maxie Rosenbloom, Rocky Graziano, Tony Zale, Jake La Motta, Marcel Cerdan, Marcel Thil, Rocky Marciano, John Henry Lewis, Billy Conn, Archie Moore, Ike Williams, Joe Brown and many more. I saw some pretty outstanding British fighters too – Len Harvey, Tommy Farr, Jack Petersen, Jack Kid Berg, Nel Tarleton, Jack Hood, Benny Lynch, Peter Kane, Jackie Brown, Jock McAvoy, Eric Boon, Ronnie James, and later Dave Charnley, Howard Winstone, Freddie Mills, Bruce Woodcock, Randolph Turpin, Don Cockell, Henry Cooper, Ken Buchanan, Terry Downes, Alan Minter, John Conteh, John H. Stracey, Jim Watt, Walter McGowan, Freddie Gilroy, John Caldwell, Alan Rudkin. It would take pages to name them all. It has been very difficult to pick out only a few. In making my selection, the fact that a boxer won a world title did not mean that I automatically rated him above an earlier fighter of the same weight who did not become a world champion. Much depends on the opposition at the time, and the opportunity of winning a title is five times easier today than twenty-five or more years ago.

The careers of some fighters were cut short through injury or in some cases through their own fault. John Conteh, for instance, seemed set to make millions after winning the world light-heavyweight crown but, with a combination of bad luck with a broken hand and a few lost weekends when he admitted going on the booze and even dabbling with cocaine, threw it all away. Like Turpin, John realized too late that the clock can never be turned back, but, unlike the unhappy Turpin, Conteh has survived and is anxious to make a go of life in retirement.

Jack Petersen retired prematurely at twenty-five because he was prone to cuts round the eyes. He had won both the light-heavy and heavyweight titles at twenty and brought a new dash and excitement to British boxing, but, tall and slender, he lacked the weight to tackle a Louis or Baer and lost three times to the heavier Walter Neusel of Germany. Petersen never weighed more than 12 st 12 lb in his fighting career. He still takes a tremendous interest in boxing as vice-president of the British Boxing Board of Control.

By contrast, Don Cockell had to battle against putting on weight. As a light-heavyweight Don seemed set to win a world title but the weight piled on until he suddenly found himself approaching 15 stone without the correct build to take the extra weight. Despite this handicap he won the British heavyweight crown and beat rated Americans Roland LaStarza and Harry Matthews (three times). He was unwisely matched against Marciano and, though brave, took a hammering for nine rounds which virtually finished him as a fighter. Without his weight problems Cockell would have become a super-champion. Luck was never kind to Don. He died from cancer soon after turning fifty.

Among the many current champions today two stand out as likely to go into boxing's Hall of Fame – Marvin Hagler and Don Curry.

I have named a galaxy of stars seen in a lifetime at the ringside. Who was the greatest of them all? For me it has to be Sugar Ray Robinson. I have not seen quite the combination of rhythm, skill and punching power since he was at his peak. He began as a fantastic welterweight and became a middleweight extraordinary. The middleweight division has produced some magnificent champions like Stanley Ketchel, Harry Greb, Mickey Walker, Tony Zale, Rocky Graziano, Marcel Cerdan, Jake La Motta, Carlos Monzon and Marvin Hagler, but I place Robinson above them all.

Sugar Ray Robinson

The greatest pound-for-pound champion I watched was Sugar Ray Robinson. I was convinced of that even as a young scribe and a devoted disciple of Joe Louis. Robinson, who won the welterweight title and the middleweight crown on five separate occasions, the last time a few weeks before his thirty-eighth birthday, battled in 201 contests between 1940 and 1965. He lost nineteen bouts but a dozen of these occurred when he had turned forty; he carried on boxing after having blown $4 million. In his first twelve years as a pro he dropped only two decisions – to Jake La Motta and Randolph Turpin. He beat them both in returns – La Motta five times, a fact which caused the Raging Bull to wisecrack, 'I fought Sugar Ray so often I should have got diabetes!' In the late seventies, when the New York boxing writers conducted a poll to nominate the best fighter of all time, Robinson came top with a 4-1 majority, with Ali second and Louis third. I would put Robinson first and Louis second, a short head in front of Ali.

The legend of Sugar Ray Robinson began when he was a teenager and attending but not taking part in a tournament at Waterbury, Connecticut. He had been born Walker Smith Junior in Detroit and was not certain whether he wanted to be a fighter or a dancer. Fight manager George Gainford was trying to persuade him to become a boxer and had taken him to the tournament. One of the competitors did not show up and Gainford volunteered his protégé as a substitute. The snag was that Walker Smith was not licensed and did not possess the necessary Amateur Athletic Union Card. So Gainford borrowed a licence from another black youngster named Ray Robinson and Walker Smith put on the best performance of the night. He stuck to the borrowed name and the real Robinson was forgotten. The 'Sugar' was added when a boxing writer turned to Gainford and said, 'Gee, George, that young fighter of yours is sweet . . . sweet as sugar.'

Robinson ran through the amateurs and was unbeaten in 125 contests. Of eighty-nine registered bouts he won sixty-eight by knockout. In 1939 he took the Golden Gloves featherweight championship and the lightweight in 1940. It was time to turn professional, but because he and Gainford were short of cash they did a deal with a wealthy beer magnate, Kurt Horrman, who became Robinson's manager and paid him regular wages. But this great fighter was not easy to handle. By twenty he had beaten top men like Sammy Angott, Fritzie Zivic, Marty Servo and Maxie Shapiro; he was flash and hitting the high spots, buying tuxedos and fast cars. This led to frequent quarrels with Horrman and Gainford and the fighter bought the contract for £2500.

Robinson invested his purses in real estate and formed Ray Robinson Enterprises, which owned a couple of dozen apartments, a barber's shop, a dry cleaner's, a bar and restaurant and a lingerie shop run by his wife. By 1950 he was worth half a million dollars. In a chauffeur-driven fuschia-coloured Cadillac, Robinson stopped the London traffic when he arrived from Paris in 1951 for the fight with Randolph Turpin. His luggage – 100 suitcases – followed, plus a line-up of characters: Bang Bang Womber (chief sparring partner), Shelton Oliver (golf professional), Roger Simons (personal barber to keep the kinks away), June Clark (male secretary), Pee Wee Beale (trainer). Honey Brewer (assistant trainer), Jimmy Karoubi (36 inches dwarf from a circus), George Gainford (manager) and two women – Edna Mae (his wife) and Evelyn (his sister).

The fight was set for July 1951. Robinson had not intended to defend his title in Europe. He had been taking a holiday, combined with a publicity tour to help pay his income tax, boxing in Paris, Zurich, Antwerp, Liège, Berlin and Turin, and was reported to be having a good time. Jack Solomons took a gamble and flew to Paris, offering Robinson £28,000 to put his title up against the inexperienced Turpin. It must have seemed like a piece of cake for Sugar Ray, but he had not reckoned with the British fighter's unusual strength and had underestimated what his good time in Europe had taken out of him. He did not discover the truth till halfway through the bout and the boxing world was shocked when Turpin took the title.

Robinson and Gainford had insisted that, in the unlikely case of defeat, the British champion must give Ray a return fight within ninety days in New York. Robinson was in better shape when they met again sixty-four days later and was leading on points when his left brow was badly split in round 10. Blood gushed out and Robinson was alarmed as the fight suddenly swung in Turpin's favour. But he reacted like a real champion, throwing a desperate right, and Turpin revealed his lack of experience, leaving himself wide open. The punch landed on his jaw and he went over backwards. He did well to beat the count and retreated to the ropes where he bobbed and weaved, avoiding many of the thirty-one punches it was estimated Sugar tossed in the next 25 seconds. Only 8 seconds of the round remained and Turpin was still on his feet but referee Ruby Goldstein halted the contest and Robinson was champion again.

By 1952 Robinson retained his title, beating Bobo Olson and Rocky Graziano, and made a bid for Joey Maxim's light-heavyweight crown. It was a night I shall always remember because it took place in one of New York's worst heat waves. With the extra powerful lights put up for the television coverage it was 104 degrees ringside at Yankee Stadium. My shirt was wringing wet and the green paint on the press benches stuck to my trousers. Women who arrived looking like Hollywood beauties became embarrassed as their mascara ran amok. The only man who looked comfortable was General Douglas MacArthur, recalled from Korea by President Truman.

Robinson had weighed in at 11 st $3\frac{1}{2}$ lb, well inside the middleweight limit. Maxim was 12 st 5 lb. Sugar Ray went a-dancing, jabbing and retreating to take the first six rounds against the light-heavyweight champion. Maxim, durable and strong, was just a plodder. It was odds on Sugar as he took the seventh but we were surprised to see him flop on to the stool. The heat was getting to him, his legs were not dancing any more. He carried on but Maxim was looking much the stronger.

At the start of round 10 Ruby Goldstein grabbed a phial of smelling salts and warned an official that he might not be able to continue as referee. As a weary Robinson returned to his corner, Goldstein literally staggered and was replaced by Ray Miller. This suited Maxim because Miller was not so quick to break up the clinches, and Joey sank more and more blows to Robinson's wasp-like mid-section. Robinson was still ahead when the thirteenth round started, but could not stand up to the body pummelling. Maxim kept going in like a tank. The exhausted Sugar threw a desperate right, missed, crashed face downwards and struggled to get to his feet. The bell sounded, and although Gainford tried to revive him and send him out he couldn't get off the stool. For the only time in his long career he failed to finish.

Robinson announced his retirement, but two-and-a-half-years later, at thirty-three, he was back and winning the middleweight title again from Bobo Olson. He lost it to Gene Fullmer but regained it with a spectacular knockout. He lost it once more to Camen Basilio, but the wonderman regained it from Basilio when nearly thirty-seven.

When nearly forty he narrowly lost his title to Paul Pender and lost again in the return, yet he was able to hold Gene Fullmer, the National Boxing Association champion, to a draw. He dropped eleven points decisions, including two fights in England, against Terry Downes and Mick Leahy, but neither man would claim they could have beaten him in his golden years.

It was a pity that Robinson, who grossed $4 million, should have had to go on fighting until he was forty-five. The night he won his first professional bout in 1940, his idol Henry Armstrong lost the last of his three titles to Fritzie Zivic on the same bell. Sugar said, 'That won't ever happen to me. I shall quit at the top.' Happily, he never became a bum and helped to start the Sugar Ray Robinson Foundation for underprivileged children in Los Angeles in 1969. The last time I met him he was not exactly affluent, but he was thrilled to tell me that, on his last visit to London, a Cockney cabby had said 'You're Sugar Ray Robinson, ain't you? I saw you fight Turpin. This ride is on me champ.' That made the best pound-for-pound fighter of the past half century a happy man.

On a less happy note, I was saddened to read recently that Robinson was suffering from Alzheimer's disease, a form of senile dementia.

Joe Louis

The most exciting heavyweight package to arrive since the young Dempsey came from the West was Joe Louis. In the thirties he gave the division a transfusion after an anaemic decade. He was not only an excellent fighter but a good citizen and a much needed ambassador for his race as America was still rife with prejudice, determined not to have another Jack Johnson as the white man's boss. Henry Wills, a competent black heavyweight, had never been allowed to challenge Dempsey. So when young Joe Louis Barrow arrived in Detroit from Alabama as a heavyweight hope, he had not only to beat every opponent but also the colour of his skin.

No heavyweight has a better record. He reigned supreme from 1937 to 1949, defending his title a record twenty-five times. Though slow on his feet compared with Ali, he delivered his combination punches faster than any other heavyweight and was a much harder hitter. Ali moved fast, Louis punched fast.

Louis was born amid the cotton fields of Lexington on 13 May 1914, the seventh child of Munroe and Lily Barrow. His father died when he was ten. His mother remarried a widower, Pat Brooks, and the combined families moved to Detroit. Joe was simple and sincere. He brought a lump to the throat of 18,000 politicians and showbiz personalities during the last war when a boxing tournament was staged at Madison Square Garden for the US Navy Relief Society. The politicians and Hollywood stars did their usual spouting but it was Joe who brought the house down, ducking under the ropes and, as the mike was thrust at him, muttering, 'We've all got to play our part and then we'll win. 'Cos we're on God's side.'

The Brown Bomber was not an immediate success as an amateur and was knocked down seven times in three rounds by Johnny Miller in his first contest. He was only seventeen but his courage was unmistakable. He lost only four of fifty-eight contests and won a Golden Gloves title in 1934. As a professional, Louis was knocked down ten times, but only two men kept him down, Max Schmeling when Louis was twenty-two and Rocky Marciano when he was thirty-seven.

He turned professional after the Golden Gloves win at the age of twenty. In one year he won twenty contests – eighteen by knockout. Six weeks after his twenty-first birthday he was matched with the giant Primo Carnera, a year after the Italian lost the title to Max Baer. Joe flattened him in six rounds. He then dismissed King Levinsky and Baer and was matched with the German Schmeling, his third former heavyweight champion opponent, in June 1936. Forty-two thousand turned up at Yankee Stadium. The Brown Bomber was hot favourite but the experienced German turned in one of his best performances and exposed young Louis as a hard-hitting novice. By occasionally leading with his right, Schmeling had Louis confused, and he put him down in the fourth round. By the tenth session Schmeling was completely in charge and Joe was hammered to the canvas in the twelfth. He was too exhausted to rise. It was his first defeat as a professional.

It was the biggest upset since Jim Braddock dethroned Baer. Nobody was more shaken than promoter Mike Jacobs, successor to Tex Rickard. He had done a deal tying Louis up for the rest of his fighting life, and with Hitler's Nazis already persecuting the Jews, Jacobs, understandably, did not want a German heavyweight champion. Within two months of defeat Joe was back flattening yet another former heavyweight champion, Jack Sharkey, then almost thirty-four. Schmeling had signed to fight Braddock for the title and turned up at Madison Square Garden for a synthetic weigh-in, but as Braddock did not put in an appearance reporters referred to it as a fight for the phantom heavyweight championship.

Braddock and his manager Joe Gould, realizing that the champion was likely to be beaten by Schmeling or Louis, did a deal with Jacobs for Braddock to meet Louis providing that, if

Joe won the title, both fighters would collect a small percentage of every Louis purse in the future. Joe remained champion for twelve years after knocking out Braddock in eight rounds at Chicago in June 1937.

The Brown Bomber's first defence came as a surprise to America. Mike Jacobs was determined to keep Schmeling out and cabled Tommy Farr, due to meet Schmeling in London, offering him a crack at Louis. The Welshman grabbed the opportunity and, nine weeks after the Braddock fight, gave the champion a terrific challenge for fifteen rounds.

Louis knocked out Nathan Mann and Harry Thomas in 1938. The only big box-office draw now was a bout with Schmeling because Farr had lost to Braddock and Baer. Joe was confident he could now beat Schmeling and was anxious for a chance to avenge his humiliating defeat two years earlier. They signed to meet at Yankee Stadium in June and 70,000 fans paid $1,015,012. It was a grudge fight. Never before had Louis revealed such emotion and dislike of an opponent. He pounced from his corner at the first bell and landed two sharp left jabs to Schmeling's face, followed by a vicious left hook to the body which made Schmeling wince. As the German backed on to the ropes, the champion in tigerish mood sunk lefts and rights to head and body and the German slid to the floor. He stumbled up completely bewildered at three, to be sent crashing a second and a third time. The demoralized German, swaying on the ropes, turned his back, but Joe was hyped for the kill and showed no mercy as he landed merciless body blows. Schmeling was later to claim he had been fouled by kidney punches. It was mayhem and all over in 2 minutes 4 seconds. It was estimated Louis threw forty punches and all but three found their target in the most punishing one-sided first round since Dempsey massacred Willard. The disgraced German was taken from the ring on a stretcher to hospital. He had to cry foul to escape some of the fury of Hitler, who had sent Max good wishes before the fight.

Louis defended his title another thirteen times before being extended in 1941 when facing Billy Conn, the young Irish light-heavyweight champion from Pittsburgh, six months before Japan attacked Pearl Harbor. Conn nearly caused a sensation by outspeeding and outboxing the champion for twelve rounds.

Billy became overconfident and started carrying the fight to Louis in the thirteenth. Few men had been able to trade punches with Joe and the Irishman was knocked out in the same round. In 1942 the champion knocked out two previous victims, Buddy Baer and Abe Simon, donating both purses to the Army and Navy Relief Funds. As a GI he gave exhibitions throughout America, Europe and the Far East.

With the war over, Mike Jacobs saw a return with Conn as the big attraction. He charged $100 ringside for the first time and 42,000 paid a total of $1,925,564, the largest receipts since the second Dempsey–Tunney bout. The fight itself flopped. Louis had put on weight and had slowed up. Conn had gone even softer and showed none of his old confidence. He scarcely threw a serious punch and was flattened in round 8. It was one of the most disappointing fights I have watched. In 1947 Louis defended against the veteran Jersey Joe Walcott. He was slipping rapidly. Walcott floored him twice and Joe was lucky to get the decision, but in the rematch in 1948 Walcott learned, like others, that Joe never made the same mistake twice. Walcott was knocked out in eleven rounds.

The Brown Bomber realized his best days were over and, after a series of exhibitions, announced his retirement on 1 March 1949. He had grossed nearly $5 million and had donated two big purses to war charities but, ironically, the old champion was a victim of financial mismanagement. He did not realize he owed tax and was heavily in debt to the US Government. And so the inevitable comeback. It was a sombre experience to see him lose a points decision to Ezzard Charles in 1950. The teeth and claws of the tiger were no longer sharp. Yet the ageing Louis carried on fighting in order to pay his debts and was still good enough to beat the likes of Cesar Brion, Freddie Beshore, Omelio Agramonte, Jimmy Bivins and Lee Savold. Savold had looked a tough battler as he cut up Bruce Woodcock in four rounds at the White City in London in a fight billed for the vacant world heavyweight championship following Louis's retirement. Yet old Joe bounced Savold round like a child before putting him away in six rounds. He greeted me as I walked into his dressing room with, 'Hey, man. Now I'm the champion of the British Empire!'

Still in need of cash, Joe took on the undefeated Marciano.

Joe was thirty-four and had been boxing seventeen years. He was balding and at least 14 lb overweight. He did well for seven rounds, cutting Rocky's nose and eyes, but with ten years against him the result was inevitable. With a series of short blows, Rocky hammered Joe to the ropes and a left and a right cross put the old man down. Referee Ruby Goldstein spared the formality of counting him out and tough New Yorkers had lumps in their throats at the passing of a super-champion who had lost only three of sixty-six contests.

Henry Armstrong

Only one fighter held three world championships at different weights at the same time. Henry Armstrong's unique achievement was the more remarkable because it happened in the thirties when there were only eight weight divisions and, with few exceptions, only eight recognized world champions. Armstrong won titles from undisputed and outstanding champions, Petey Sarron (featherweight, 9 st), Lou Ambers (light, 9 st 9 lb) and Barney Ross (welter, 10 st 7 lb). All were won between October 1937 and August 1938. No wonder he was known as Homicide Hank.

He was born Henry Jackson on a cotton plantation in Columbus, Mississippi, in 1912, the eleventh of fifteen children of two sharecroppers who were virtually slaves. His mother was mostly Cherokee Indian, his father a mixture of Negro and Irish. At that time there were still public whippings and the occasional lynching for blacks. What was there for a black kid to do in the Deep South other than to shine shoes, sell papers and fight? But even when the family moved to St Louis he received little help. The first manager he approached to help him in the gymnasium shouted, 'I don't handle niggers!' An old light-heavyweight named Harry Armstrong took a liking to the kid and showed him a few tricks in the gym. When he began fighting as a teenager his mentor suggested he took the name Melody Jackson. He seldom picked up more than $2 a time and was not allowed to meet a white opponent in St Louis. So Harry took him off to California. Without any cash, it was a question of hitch-hiking and sleeping rough and living on the fruit they plucked from orchards. In desperation he took on his first pro fight with two broken ribs when sick from lack of food. He was knocked out in three rounds. He changed his name to Henry Armstrong and for five years took part in two or three fights a month, sometimes twice a week. He was poorly paid but it was the only way he could eat, and though he won more bouts than he lost, it was not until 1937 that he was given recognition and a fight in New York. In that year alone he had twenty-seven contests, winning them all, twenty-six by knockout, including the world featherweight championship by beating Petey Sarron in six rounds.

It was only when he teamed up with Eddie Mead, a 17-stone New Yorker, that his fame spread, but Eddie, a likable hustler, grossly overworked the willing fighter, as had all his previous handlers.

Mead had tremendous contacts and was able to talk Al Jolson into a $5000 deal as manager of the sensational fighter from the Deep South. Mead remained the real manager but Jolson, the Broadway and Hollywood singing star, enjoyed the publicity. Seven months after beating Sarron, Henry was matched with Barney Ross, the welter king, and scored a sensational victory. Ten weeks later, he won his third world crown, outpointing Lou Ambers. In 1940 he was unlucky not to get more than a draw against the National Boxing Association middleweight champion Ceferino Garcia, which would have given him four titles. As it was, Henry caused boxing legislators to change their rules to prevent a super-champion retaining more than one championship at a time.

In May 1939 Armstrong and Mead came to London to defend the welter title against British champion Ernie Roderick. Mead thrived on publicity and the boxing writers were given a story every day. I was allowed to sit in Armstrong's dressing room half an hour before the fight while Henry slept as peacefully as a young baby. He was awakened and went into the most vigorous shadow-boxing display I have seen in a dressing room. Beginning slowly, he worked up to a crescendo, with perspiration dripping from him after fifteen minutes. 'The kid's got a slow heartbeat,' said Mead. 'He needs to get warmed up before he gets into the ring. He'll go on throwing punches all night.'

How right Mead was. After winning a short argument about

the amount of bandage he was allowed to wear on each hand, Henry was ready to go. I noticed how badly shaped his knuckles were as well as all the scars around his eyes from the glut of fights he had taken part in since 1931.

He danced and shadow-boxed all the way to the ringside. After weighing up Roderick in the first round he put on a display of perpetual motion, throwing hundreds of punches for the next fourteen rounds to take an easy decision from the brave but outclassed British champion. It was to Roderick's credit that he stayed the distance.

Armstrong was not a knockout puncher, but a destructive hitter who wore down most of his opponents. His lack of skill cost him the lightweight title when he met Ambers again. The decision went against him only because of rounds taken away for careless low blows. And his complete lack of defence brought more and more scars as he fought on until 1945. He had taken part in 174 recorded professional contests and many more not listed. He once estimated he had had more than 260 contests.

After losing the welter title to Fritzie Zivic in 1941, Armstrong fought on for five years. Despite his success, he had not saved. Mead was a compulsive gambler who could not resist the horses. He always had cash problems. Shortly after the phenomenal fighter lost the last of his triple crowns, Mead dropped dead from a heart attack. The only winner he had backed was Henry Armstrong, but that fortune had vanished.

Archie Moore

There will never be another Archie Moore. His record is almost unbelievable. He won 199 of 234 recorded contests and fought many more not listed. He scored 145 knockouts, and boxed for nearly thirty years. He had passed thirty-nine before given a crack at the world cruiserweight championship and retained it when he was forty-eight. The Old Mongoose, as he was sometimes called, held on to his crown for a decade and never lost it in the ring. He boxed for the last time when turned fifty. If we accept his mother's claim that he was three years older than he admitted, he knocked out an unknown warrior in Phoenix in three rounds at the age of fifty-three!

Born at Benoit, Mississippi, a victim of a broken family, he was brought up by an aunt in St Louis. Inevitably he got into trouble as a kid and spent twenty-two months in a Missouri state reformatory. He showed skill and power in the gymnasium but for the first sixteen years of his career he hit opponents too hard for his own good. He was bad news, someone to avoid, and without the right connections he made little progress and earned even less cash. So in 1940 he took up an offer to go to Australia where he won all his seven fights.

A remarkable feat of Moore's life is his battle against bad health. On returning from Australia, he collapsed in the street in San Diego and was rushed to hospital and operated on immediately for a perforated ulcer, remaining on the danger list for five days. He was kept in hospital nearly six weeks and his weight dropped from 160 lb to 110 lb. The doctors warned him he would not be able to carry on fighting. Yet within twelve months he was back in the ring and in 1942 scored five knockouts, a points decision and one draw. But he was still fighting in small towns for peanuts. All the champions were avoiding him.

His record was eventually noticed by Jimmy Johnston, the New York manager known as the Boy Bandit and closely connected with Madison Square Garden. In five months and seven bouts under Johnston, Moore earned more than in the previous eight years. When Johnston died in his sleep in 1946 his brother Charlie inherited Archie. Charlie lacked the Boy Bandit's flair and Moore found himself fighting in South America when all he wanted was a crack at the title.

The New York boxing writers took up his case. They demanded he be matched with Joey Maxim for the championship, which Maxim had won from Freddie Mills in London. Maxim was managed by cagey Doc Kearns, who had been behind Dempsey and Mickey Walker. The Doc knew Moore would win, so he demanded $100,000 for Maxim; Archie ended up borrowing $10,000 from Charlie Johnston to pay his expenses to meet Maxim in 1952. Kearns and Johnston also did a deal cutting the Doc in on the future management of Moore. Eventually Charlie sold the contract to Kearns. As expected, Moore gave Maxim a sound beating over fifteen rounds, thus achieving what he could have accomplished many years earlier if he had been given the chance. Because of the Kearns–Johnston tie-up, Maxim fought two more losing title bouts with Moore.

An extraordinary side to Archie Moore was his ability to shed weight regularly, even in his forties; he would lose as much as 30 lb or more. He was a dedicated dieter and often trained in a plastic track suit to sweat off the pounds, but, remarkably, he always seemed strong at the weight. With his tongue in his cheek, Archie claimed that when in Australia he had been given a secret diet by an Aborigine witch doctor. This was all good fun for publicity purposes, but Archie had seriously studied health diets in Australia.

Even after becoming champion, Moore could not earn the sort of cash Marciano and Sugar Ray Robinson were picking up and he asked Kearns to get him a shot at Marciano's heavyweight title. But first he had to eliminate Nino Valdes, a more than useful Cuban contender. Then came another health blow. He was due to meet Frankie Daniels in a warm-up affair in San Diego but the doctor of the Californian Commission found a heart disorder and sent him to hospital for investigation.

For the second time in his career doctors informed Moore he must not fight again. Neither Moore nor Kearns accepted the findings as final and Archie went to see heart specialists in Chicago who confirmed that he had a heart murmur. And so to the Ford Hospital in Detroit with a good result. The hospital decided he did not have an organic ailment but an irregular rhythm that could be treated. A cardiograph cleared him and he took a decision off Valdes to clinch the Marciano match. Archie was knocked out in nine rounds but only after putting Rocky on the deck in the first round with a great right hand. After beating Yolande Pompey in London, he was given a second crack at the heavyweight title. Marciano had retired and Archie met Floyd Patterson for the title. But Moore failed again as a heavyweight and was knocked out in the fifth.

As a light-heavyweight Archie was invincible, he seemed to get more deadly with age. He was forty-five when he defended the title against Yvon Durelle, a French-Canadian fisherman, at Montreal. Durelle, fifteen years younger than Moore, nearly caused an upset when he caught the champion cold in the first round, putting him down three times, and again in the fifth. But the Old Mongoose recovered, put the fisherman down in the seventh and tenth and knocked him out in the eleventh. When they met again eight months later Archie put Durelle down four times in round 3 before knocking him out.

Ancient Archie dropped a decision to Giulio Rinaldi in Rome in 1960. He was not in good shape for this non-title affair and was fined $1000 for weighing $190\frac{1}{4}$ lb, but when defending the championship against Rinaldi at Madison Square Garden eight months later Moore, 16 lb lighter, retained the title. He never lost the championship in the ring but made the mistake of thinking he could tame an up-and-coming young heavyweight named Cassius Clay who stopped him in four rounds.

As a light-heavyweight Archie was supreme. His illness, his ability to lose weight and his endurance in defying the march of time made him a ring phenomenon. How can there ever be another fighter quite like Archie Moore.

Rocky Marciano

Rocco Francesco Marchegiano was a throwback to the granite age, chiselled from indestructible rock like Dempsey. He was not a giant, standing but 5 ft 10 in and scaling only 184 lb, with the shortest reach of any heavyweight champion, but his record is unique because in nine years as a professional he was never beaten or held to a draw. Tunney was the only other heavyweight champion who retired with his crown and was not persuaded to come back. Marciano must be listed with Dempsey, Louis and Max Baer among the hardest-hitting champions.

His father, a cobbler, left Italy with his wife Pasqualina before the First World War and settled at Brockton in Massachusetts. Rocky was one of six children. He was yet another street-fighting kid and did not try on a pair of boxing gloves until joining the army in the war. He was in the 150th Combat Engineers along with his school pal Al Colombo and spent some time in England and Wales. He was a crude but indestructible fighter and nearly always demolished the other guy. When demobbed in 1946 he joined an amateur club and in twenty-seven bouts lost only one decision, to Coley Wallace. He was offered a few dollars to fight a professional named Lee Epperson and, using the name of Rocky Mack, knocked the pro out in three rounds. That decided it. He became a full-time professional and was known as Rocky Marciano.

Al Colombo stuck with him as friend and adviser and in 1948 Rocky flattened his first eleven opponents, eight in the first round and two in the second; one guy lasted three rounds. The following year he won another thirteen bouts, eleven by knockout, but he was not making a fortune. He was twenty-six. Colombo did not know the big boys of boxing so he wrote to Al Weill, a tough manager and matchmaker at Madison Square Garden. Weill had been in charge of some famous fighters and was unimpressed by Rocky's crude style, but trainer Charlie Goldman, born in London, said to Weill, 'The guy's as hard as granite and hurts whenever he can land a punch. Maybe we can teach him something.' Weill, a tough businessman, was only interested if, in the event of Rocky getting top matches, the purse was split 50-50. Goldman was unable to polish Marciano's defence but was amazed at his power and told Weill there was not a guy living who could beat him. He proved correct.

Marciano was not as dumb as his critics made out. He had short arms, but when onlookers thought he was missing he was deliberately making a target of his opponent's arms and biceps. Once badly bruised, they had to drop their arms, and then Marciano always got his man. He took the ageing Louis in eight rounds and then quickly polished off Lee Savold, Gino Buonvino, Bernie Reynolds and Harry Matthews. He was ready to challenge Jersey Joe Walcott for the heavyweight crown in Philadelphia in September 1952.

Jersey Joe was a master boxer and a pretty good puncher; though nearly thirty-nine, he was confident he could outbox the crude, swinging Rocky. This he did in the opening round, dropping and cutting Marciano, who had never been down before. Walcott continued to outbox and punish Rocky. The challenger's right brow was split, his left eye half closed, his lips puffed and bleeding, and more blood dripped from a gash in his forehead. Charlie Goldman told him at the end of the twelfth that only a knockout could save him. He came out like a wounded bull in round 13 and forced the tiring Walcott on to the ropes. Then he released a combination of short punches, the right finally landing on Walcott's jaw, twisting his face as though it were a rubber mask. The blood drained from Jersey Joe as he sank down and out. It was one of the best final punches in a heavyweight championship. Marciano's face was cut to pulp but at the age of twenty-nine he had become the first white heavyweight king since Braddock.

The return clause in all contracts involving world titles still ruled in America and the pair were due to meet again the following April, but when I arrived at Chicago Stadium to collect my press ticket I was told the fight had been postponed a month: Rocky had suffered a nose haemorrhage that very day while sparring at his training camp. So it was straight back to London. When they met in May 1953 Marciano did not have to worry about his nose. Walcott had lost all his old confidence, remembering how hard Rocky had hit him in Philadelphia. He back-pedalled and Marciano immediately attacked. Jersey Joe's response was feeble and Rocky forced him on the ropes and released half a dozen punches. Walcott collapsed. He got to one knee but was counted out. He later claimed he had misjudged the count. It was all over in 2 minutes 25 seconds.

Rocky marched on beating Roland LaStarza (eleven rounds) Ezzard Charles (fifteen and eight rounds), Don Cockell (nine rounds) and Archie Moore (nine rounds). Though never defeated as a professional, his lack of defence cost him plenty in spilled blood. Only his bull-like strength and courage kept his record intact. The postponement of the Walcott fight was the first warning and during the first Ezzard Charles affair, his nose seemed almost to have split in half. Moore dropped him in the first round. He could still have taken Floyd Patterson and Ingemar Johansson but on 27 April 1956 he announced his retirement. He was thirty-two and had decided to sit back and enjoy his share of $1½ million grossed from seven title bouts. On 1 August 1969 he was flying in a private plane to celebrate his forty-sixth birthday the following day, but died when the plane crashed at Newton, Iowa. I attended his requiem mass at the Italian Church in London's Clerkenwell. Many champions attended to remember the Rock who could only be beaten by death.

Sugar Ray Leonard

A detached retina of his left eye robbed Sugar Ray Leonard of the possibility of overtaking the original Sugar Ray as the greatest pound-for-pound boxer. As a fighting man he was cut down in his prime at twenty-six, with only one defeat in thirty-four contests over eight years. Robinson took part in 201 bouts, winning 174 in a career spanning a quarter of a century. Yet the sheer magic of Leonard's moves made him the biggest name in boxing after Ali and bigger at the box office than Ali's successor as heavyweight king, Larry Holmes. Up to this time the heavyweight champion had always outstripped the most brilliant of lighter pugilists when it came to moneyspinners. Only Leonard's premature retirement allowed Marvin Hagler to grab the boxing headlines and the millions that go with them.

Leonard had been groomed by American television to be a star even before he had proved himself as a professional. He was acclaimed a golden boy at twenty, winning an Olympic Games title at Montreal in 1976, having won 145 of 150 amateur contests, seventy-five by knockout. Less arrogant than Robinson, Ali or Wilfredo Benitez, Leonard's image was moulded as a nice guy who did everything correctly. After winning the Olympic gold medal, he declared that, now his ambition had been realized, he would retire from boxing and study at the University of Maryland. CBS Television had other ideas. They saw him as something to be packaged on the small screen. Leonard was persuaded to change his idealistic resolution which I am sure he had intended to keep as he stood on the Olympic rostrum with tears of emotion in his eyes as the US national anthem was heard yet again.

His change of heart was understandable. His father was sick. His mother, a nurse, had suffered a minor heart attack. Though not married, he had a three-year-old son. He needed the cash. So he sought the counsel of his oldest friend, Janks Morton, who had helped train him. Morton introduced him to a wealthy and trusted friend, Mike Trainer, a Maryland attorney.

Mike was impressed by the boxer's skill in the Olympics and by his demeanour outside the ropes. So he formed a syndicate of twenty-four business friends who invested $20,000 to underwrite Leonard's professional career with the promise they would all be repaid within four years plus 8 per cent interest. In the meantime the boxer drew $900 a month from Sugar Ray Leonard Incorporated as exclusive stockholder. CBS immediately signed him as a television boxing commentator. Sponsors and advertising agents were anxious to purchase his name and he was inundated with invitations to speak at dinners and open carnivals. He was even offered a part in a film before his first professional contest.

Angelo Dundee, who had won fame as Ali's trainer and cornerman, signed to work with and advise Leonard for 15 per cent of his earnings. Angelo selected the first opponent carefully. He chose a durable Puerto Rican, Luis the Bull Vega. Leonard collected the decision and $40,000 for this carefully planned launching at Baltimore in February 1977. The Leonard PRO organization did not miss a trick. A telegram was sent to the White House inviting President Carter to attend but pointing out if he had other business he could always tune in to CBS.

In the next three years Leonard won all his twenty-five contests. He had become such an attraction that he could demand $200,000 per match against non-championship opposition. He had natural skill, but he also rehearsed the Ali shuffle and, with the help of Dundee, imitated other Ali gimmicks, By 1979 he was ready to take on the highly skilled Wilfred Benitez for the WBC welter championship and after a terrific fight handed out Benitez's first defeat, stopping him in the fifteenth round.

Then came the big upset: losing the title to Duran in a punishing fifteen-round brawl at Montreal and 'psyching' his conqueror in New Orleans five months afterwards. Those two fights were worth around $17 million to Sugar Ray. Having won a second world championship by stopping Ayub Kalule to take the junior middleweight crown, Leonard faced Thomas Hearns, the WBA welter king for the undisputed world championship. Hearns, from Detroit, known as the Hit Man, was undefeated. His clash with Leonard in Las Vegas was a tremendous showdown, attracting an estimated 300 million television viewers with receipts reported as a record $35 million, outstripping the first Leonard–Duran meeting. In a classic encounter of skilled boxing and big hitting Hearns gave Leonard plenty of trouble, including a badly bruised left eye. The majority of experts had Leonard ahead after twelve rounds but the three judges had Hearns in front. It was fortunate for Sugar Ray that he had agreed to WBA rules of fifteen rounds rather than those of the WBC, which insists on only twelve rounds for a championship. The wise old Angelo Dundee, however, was concerned and bullied Leonard in his corner at the end of round 12. 'You're blowin' the fight. Go get him!' yelled Dundee. Sugar Ray turned on the heat in the thirteenth and in the next round dropped Hearns with a hook to the jaw. The Hit Man was almost exhausted. He staggered to his feet but his legs had gone and the referee stopped the battle. Leonard proved himself a real champ by producing the lethal punch at the time of crisis, as Sugar Ray Robinson did in the second Turpin affair.

It was while preparing to defend the crown against Roger Stafford in the spring of 1982 that Leonard discovered he had a detached retina in his left eye. The fight was cancelled and an operation followed. He rested for six months before making an announcement about his future. He was only twenty-six and had grossed between $35 and $40 million and, after vast taxes and expenses, probably had $12 million invested.

Negotiations were about to begin for a possible meeting with Marvin Hagler for the undisputed middleweight crown worth another $7 or $8 million to Leonard. If successful, he would have won three world titles and would have made another $40 million before retiring. But what is the price of a man's sight? Though still young, he had been boxing since fourteen. He was now married and his son, Ray Junior, was eight. His wife

Juanita wanted him to quit. He announced his retirement at the end of 1982 and remained inactive throughout 1983, but the urge to box again was so great that eventually he agreed to a 'trial' comeback against Kevin Howard, a journeyman from Philadelphia in 1984. He postponed this match to undergo treatment to strengthen the retina of his other eye, which indicated how worried he was. Though it was a non-title fight and Howard was not reckoned to have a chance, such was the interest in Leonard's comeback that when they met in May it was worth $3 million to him and Howard was delighted to earn $125,000. It was as well Sugar Ray had opted for a trial and not taken on a top contender. He stopped Howard in nine rounds but the old magic was missing and he experienced the indignity of having to get up off the floor in round 4, the first knock-down he had experienced. He was obviously concerned about his eye, had lost much of his old confidence and was easy to hit. Within minutes of winning he announced his second retirement, this time for good. 'It just isn't there any more,' he admitted. 'I have too much pride to risk injury or humiliation. My decision was made while on the canvas. I saw the look on my wife's face and decided "This is it!" '

At twenty-eight Sugar Ray Leonard, a super-champion, accepted that boxers should never come back – not even after only two years out of the ring. I welcomed his decision to retire on a winning note and as a wealthy young man.

But the lure of the ring got to Sugar Ray almost two years to the day after he had beaten Howard and admitted: 'It just isn't there any more. I'm through.' In May, 1986, a couple of weeks before his thirtieth birthday, Leonard announced: 'I want one more fight – against Marvin Hagler for the middleweight title.' Conceding it was an ego trip, Leonard insisted he didn't want to fight anybody other than Hagler – a match that could be worth a total purse of $30 million. Though the incentive is great there will be many Leonard admirers hoping he will think again before returning to the ring.

Marvin Hagler

The PR boys call him Marvellous Marvin Hagler. Damon Runyon would have applied an even more exuberant adjective, for Hagler qualifies among the greats in a division that has produced so many super-champions. No fighter can do more than thrash all the challengers of his day. With shaven head, a menacing Fu Manchu moustache and a scowl from the Chamber of Horrors, Hagler relishes his image as the Baddest Man in Town. He will not be remembered as the hardest punching middleweight but there have not been many more damaging punchers. His left jab draws blood with the sureness of a surgeon's scalpel, as Kevin Finnegan (thirty stitches in two fights), Alan Minter (fifteen stitches) and Vito Antuofermo (forty-five stitches in two contests) will vouch. Yet despite the satanic image, he is not a brawling southpaw but an underrated graceful boxer with an intimidating reach of 75 inches.

Though I named him the Boston Ripper after all the blood he caused to flow, I found him articulate in conversation and not unfriendly outside the ropes. He is a professional and realizes it is in his own financial interest to build his reputation as an uncompromising fighter who acts mean and does not enjoy shaking an opponent's hand until he can do so as the conqueror. He was yet another black kid who lived in squalor in Newark. When the race riots there became unbearable, his mother moved to the comparative safety of Brockton, Massachusetts, birthplace of Rocky Marciano. He took to fighting but smouldered because he was never given a crack at the title until he was twenty-seven. He is a loner, dedicated to fitness, and before his toughest tests would lead a monastic way of life. He would drive to a hotel on Cape Cod and punish himself at nights in a makeshift gymnasium. Early in the morning, even in winter, when the Cape is frozen, he was on the road. Some fighters would call it masochism but by the time Hagler reported for sparring in less severe surroundings a couple of weeks later his body was as hard as iron and his mood was as mean as the icy wind. He vowed he would never be beaten by lack of condition. But he has little to grumble about financially. Since turning professional in 1973 he has grossed nearly $25 million. Marciano's total earnings were just above $1.5 million!

When he first decided boxing was the only way he could earn a living, he went as a fifteen-year-old to the gym run by the Petronelli brothers, Goody and Pat, who were kind to him. He has remained loyal to them even though he knew they did not have the political clout to get him big matches. It was agreed they should approach Steve Wainwright, an influential lawyer with the right connections. Wainwright was able to get Hagler a match at Monaco in 1979 against Norberto Cabrera, an Argentinian, fighting on the same bill as Hugo Corro, Argentina's world middleweight champion, defending his title against Vito Antuofermo.

Corro lost his title to the Italian, who was living in America, and Hagler stopped Cabrera in eight rounds. He impressed sufficiently to be given a crack at Antuofermo's new title in Las Vegas. It was a gruelling fight and most onlookers thought Hagler had done enough to get the decision, but a draw was announced and the Italian kept the title. Hagler expected a return fight but Antuofermo defended against British champion Alan Minter in Las Vegas. Minter, boxing with unusual restraint, took the decision and the crown and then gave Vito a return fight in London which the British champion won with ease. Hagler was angry at being left out, but three months later he was given the chance to face Minter at Wembley in what turned out to be a bitter contest, with the American ripping Alan's face and taking the crown in 8 minutes 45 seconds.

Though Hagler had at last proved he was the best middleweight in the world, he still carried a chip on his shoulder. Sugar Ray Leonard, the welterweight champion, had been built up by television as the Number One fight star. Hagler was hoping to get a big pay day with a clash with the welterweight champion but Leonard's eye injury brought about his premature retirement and Hagler began to take over as the big name in boxing. He easily beat seven challengers: Fulgencio Obelmejias (eight rounds), Antuofermo (four rounds), Mustafo Hamsho (eleven rounds), Caveman Lee (one round), Obelmejias (five rounds), Tony Sibson (six rounds), Wilfred Scypion (four rounds), and then collected $5.5 million against Roberto Duran, who surprisingly took him fifteen rounds. This was followed by easier defences against Juan Domingo Roldan and Hamasho again, building up to close on $8 million against Thomas Hearns, who held the WBC junior middleweight crown.

This bout lasted only three rounds but contained more action than is often seen in fifteen. The first round was three minutes of mayhem with both fighters shaking each other with a cascade of blows. Blood was pouring from a gash between Hagler's eyes with half a minute of round 1 remaining. Hagler, more used to drawing an opponent's blood than spilling his own, became even meaner as he went after Hearns, but a cut then appeared under Marvin's right eye. At the end of the second round the referee examined Hagler's wounds and midway through a brawling third round halted the bout and requested the doctor to examine Hagler's cut. It was a crisis for the Boston fighter, but the doctor allowed the contest to continue. Hagler desperately proved to be a real champion as he charged into Hearns and took him apart with a clubbing swing followed by three more crushing blows which sent the Hit Man sprawling. He bravely dragged himself off the canvas but his legs were as limp as a puppet's. The referee rightly stopped what would have become slaughter. Those three rounds of action compared with three rounds of nonstop punching between Tony Zale and Rocky Graziano in their third clash for the middleweight crown at Newark in 1948 when Zale rewon the title. And the two British middleweights, Mark Kaylor and Errol Christie, showed similar guts in their eliminator clash in 1985, with each scoring a knock-down in the opening round and Kaylor surviving a second knock-down before finally knocking out Christie in round 8.

After beating Hearns, Hagler claimed thirty-five consecutive wins and eleven defences of the title. He was then approaching thirty-one and was without doubt the best middleweight since Carlos Monzon retired undefeated champion in 1977. But it is to the credit of John Mugabi, the hard-hitting Ugandan, that he gave Marvin his toughest battle for the title in 1986. How does Hagler compare with Robinson? No middleweight can equal Sugar Ray's record over a quarter of a century. Though some of Hagler's challengers were moderate, he must be up there with Monzon, who defended his crown fourteen times in seven years, and that means he has the right to rival Jake La Motta, Marcel Cerdan and Tony Zale as one of the six best middleweights of all time.

Roberto Duran

Roberto Duran is a noble savage and was the best lightweight of the past half century. He possesses the uncompromising ferocity of Harry Greb, Rocky Graziano and Jake La Motta. I believe he would have outgunned the more stylish Ike Williams, Joe Brown and Alexis Arguello. He carved his name in the Hall of Fame, defending the 9 st 9 lb crown a dozen times and winning all but three out of sixty-three contests in this division, fifty-one inside the distance. He relinquished his championship to battle in higher divisions, becoming a champion at three separate weights, and made a splendid bid for a fourth title against the menacing middleweight king Marvin Hagler. When flattened in two rounds by Thomas Hearns while attempting to win the junior middleweight title, he was thirty-three years old and had brawled in eighty-three fights over fifteen years.

Whether sporting a moustache or a goatee beard, Duran, with his blazing Latin eyes, was a ferocious man to interview, never mind fight. He was one of the great hungry fighters brought up in a turbulent environment on the streets of La Chorrillo, some forty miles from Panama City. A born survivor, he regularly used to swim two miles to Fort Amador to raid mango and coconut trees. This amused Carlos Eleta, a former tennis champion of Panama and a millionaire, whose fruit the young roughneck regularly robbed. Eleta sponsored him, encouraged him to fight and became his adviser when he turned professional at sixteen. Ray Arcel, the veteran American trainer, was hired to add a little skill such as slipping a punch and how to jab as well as swing. Duran did most of his fighting in Panama and remained undefeated.

At twenty-one he was given his big chance to go to New York to challenge Scotland's accomplished Ken Buchanan for the world crown. The Scot was a tremendous favourite with the Madison Square Garden crowd but the sheer ferocity of the man affectionately known to his fans as El Animal and Manos de Piedra (Hands of Stone) overwhelmed Buchanan, who lost the title in the thirteenth round. The new champion went back to Panama City and painted the town red, pausing from his celebrations to knock out a couple of guys in a round apiece. He returned to Madison Square Garden somewhat overweight and dropped a decision for the first time to the Puerto Rican Esteban de Jesus in a non-title bout. But after this misadventure the man from Panama defended the crown twelve times in the next seven years, including two knockouts of de Jesus, before relinquishing it in 1979.

By 1970 Duran was having difficulty keeping to 9 st 9 lb. His target was Sugar Ray Leonard, elegant undefeated welter king. Forty-six thousand turned up at Montreal, with Sugar Ray a firm favourite, but the unbelievable *machismo* of Manos de Piedra swept aside the superior skill of Leonard from the first bell. Leonard's pride was such that instead of retaining his role as sweet scientist he went a-brawling, and nothing on two legs could get away with such tactics against the Panamanian. Despite his erroneous battle plans, Leonard fought like a true champion and lost a controversial decision. A rematch was the order, and five months later Duran defended the championship against Sugar Ray at New Orleans with the most unpredictable and inexplicable ending to any world championship contest. I deal with this extraordinary return later in the book, but Duran, after six months of rehabilitation and atonement, revealed himself as a real man of war. He lived down the sneers of so-called friends and the graffiti in his home town branding him as a 'chicken' and a 'quitter'. He was encouraged by real friends who still had faith in him and the President of Panama invited him to come home from Miami where he had become a recluse for more than a week. Seven months later he boxed a three-round exhibition in New York and was well received. He won a couple of fights and then took a crack at Wilfredo

Benitez's junior middleweight crown. He fought well though losing a fifteen-round decision to the talented Puerto Rican.

Another setback against former British champion Kirkland Laing looked like the end of the championship road. His friend and manager Carlos Eleta advised him to quit after the second Leonard bout and they ended their long relationship. Even Eleta had underestimated the determination of Roberto to prove he could still be a champion and the boxing world was staggered in 1983 when he stopped Davey Moore in eight rounds to win his third world crown – the junior middleweight. Such was his ambition that he took on Hagler for the middleweight title and, despite the prophets of doom, took the awesome Marvin the full fifteen rounds. Alas, his appetite for fighting and ambition for titles and cash were insatiable and he unwisely met Thomas Hearns, the WBC junior middleweight champion, for the undisputed title and a $3 million purse.

His best days were behind him and the lanky hard-hitting Hearns had the wrong style for a once feared brawler throwing punches into the twilight. Manos de Piedra was stretched out in two rounds. This, surely, was the end of the seventeen-year war waged by the Noble Savage who had become a legend? It seemed so when he tasted the good life and his weight rocketed to almost 16 stone. He looked like Mister Five-by-Five, but his love of fighting for the sake of fighting sent him back to the gym where he shed 55 lb. Eighteen months later, in January 1986, he made a comeback at Panama City in his thirty-fifth year. It was nearly twenty years since he had made his ring debut. He weighed in at 11 st 11 lb, his heaviest fighting weight ever. Twelve thousand fans turned up to see him knock out Colombian champion Manuel Esteban Zambrano in two rounds. He followed up with a two-round KO of Jose Suero and declared he wanted to win the middleweight crown and become the first pugilist to hold four world championships at different weights.

Idiot's delight? It will take a brave man to tell Roberto Duran he should ever give up fighting but the facts are that at thirty-five the once super lightweight is a flabby middleweight and while he sought to earn millions by going in again with Hagler for the 11 st 6 lb crown, it would not be in the best physical interests of Duran or the image of boxing. After nearly twenty years of brawling, time at last is catching up with him. This became evident on the McGuigan–Cruz bill at Las Vegas when he was narrowly outpointed by Robbie Sims, half brother of Marvin Hagler. Duran was edged out of the decision and fought with honour. But enough is enough, and I hope that boxing's most noble savage will accept this fact of his long fighting life.

Larry Holmes

If Larry Holmes had quit the ring at thirty-six, his record would have assured him of an undisputed place with the all-time greats. He had won all forty-eight fights and defended the title twenty-one times. Having grossed $56 million, he didn't need the cash but, like Ali, his ego outweighed his judgement. He wanted to equal and perhaps beat Rocky Marciano's record of success in all forty-nine fights. So though slowing down fast, he was convinced he could beat Michael Spinks, the undisputed light-heavyweight champion. His gamble failed as age and Spinks caught up with him and he lost a decision for the first time. He decided to quit but, convinced he could beat Spinks, tried again but lost a split and hotly disputed decision after nearly knocking out Spinks in the fourteenth round. He bitterly criticized the judges and declined to attend a press conference. Like so many other kings of the ring, Holmes had stayed around too long. But you can't take away that record of forty-eight successive wins before he faced Spinks.

It had not been easy to follow in the steps of the Master. Holmes had to work long and hard after Ali retired before being accepted as a worthy heavyweight champion. Perhaps he had been content too long to serve his apprenticeship as sparring partner to Joe Frazier, Jimmy Young, Earnie Shavers and Ali. How could an artisan be accepted alongside the Greatest? Furthermore Holmes became champion only on a split verdict against Ken Norton, who had been proclaimed a political champion by the WBC without throwing a punch in anger. Championships should only be won and lost in the ring, but the

WBC had decided Norton was champion following Ali's retirement in 1979. Holmes had some pretty soft defences of his title, stopping Alfredo Evangelista, Osvaldo Ocasio, Lorenzo Zanon, Leroy Jones and Scott Ledoux. He also beat Earnie Shavers and Mike Weaver, but in each case found himself on the deck first. It wasn't until two years as champion, when the extraordinary Don King tempted Ali back for a fourth attempt to win the world title at thirty-eight, that Holmes was able to rid himself of the label of Pretender.

All he really beat was the shadow of Ali. The old champion's magic had completely vanished. After drastic dieting Ali went into the ring looking as slim as in his days of glory, but he had nothing to offer. After ten rounds Angelo Dundee decided it was a lost cause and the Great Man himself was resigned to capitulating before the end of a contest for the only time in a distinguished career.

Holmes began to emerge as invincible in his own right and continued to beat the best and the worst around. His defence against Gerry Cooney, the New York Irishman, in Las Vegas in 1982 was said to be worth nearly $10 million to each of them. The 6 ft 7 in New Yorker had been wrapped in cotton wool for his title build-up. Between 1977 and 1981 he had won all of his twenty-five fights. It wasn't one of the greatest heavyweight bouts I have watched, but Cooney gave a courageous account of himself before getting stopped in the thirteenth round when his trainer Victor Valle climbed into the ring and gently put his arms round the young giant to end the pain.

Larry continued defending his title. He worked closely with Don King, who chose the challengers and named the size of the purse. Holmes was more than satisfied. On King's advice he gave up the WBC version of the championship because of a dispute over the purse and, as champion of the newly formed International Boxing Federation, chose his own challengers. He continued to be undefeated and collected immense purses, due mainly to television, but he was eventually caught in the same trap as Ali and so many past champions. He had become easy to hit against moderate challengers and was slowing up fast when he chose as his challenger Michael Spinks, the undefeated light-heavyweight champion.

On paper this appeared an easy defence for Holmes. No

light-heavyweight champion had ever taken the title away from a heavyweight king. Georges Carpentier, Tommy Loughran, John Henry Lewis, Billy Conn, Archie Moore and Bob Foster had all learned the lesson that a good big 'un usually beats a good little 'un. Victory over Spinks would have put Holmes on equal terms with Marciano and one more easy defence would have set him up for life as an all-time great. What Larry had forgotten is that there are no easy fights after thirty. He had pressed his luck too far. Spinks, six years his junior, used speed to cancel out Larry's weight advantage. A slow and cumbersome heavyweight champion was outpointed.

In going after Marciano's record, Holmes enabled Michael Spinks to set up two new records. Spinks was the first reigning light-heavyweight champion to beat a heavyweight champion. It was also the first time two brothers had won the heavyweight crown, his older brother Leon Spinks having taken the title off Ali in 1978 only to lose it back to the Greatest six months later. The brothers had each won Olympic Gold medals at Montreal in 1976.

Alexis Arguello

Alexis Arguello is indeed a man. He has handled triumph and disaster. A super fighter from troubled Nicaragua, he became one of seven pugilists to win three world titles – featherweight, junior lightweight and lightweight – and never lost one in the ring. His world suddenly fell apart when at the age of thirty he made a bid for a fourth crown against the brilliant junior welter champion Aaron Pryor in 1982. In a punishing battle he was stopped at the end of thirteen rounds. Not convinced Pryor was his master, he tried again a year later and ended in tears on his knees, beaten in ten rounds.

Like other great champions, he was to pay dearly for misjudging the final curtain. He had been one of the world's most respected fighters because he behaved impeccably and extended courtesy wherever he boxed. He came to Wembley to take the WBC lightweight crown from Jim Watt in the first big fight there after unfortunate crowd violence following the Hagler–Minter bout. He not only praised his beaten opponent but described British boxing fans as true sportsmen and said he would always be glad to box in Britain again, much needed reassurance after the Hagler affair.

Though a destroyer in the ring, Arguello was gentle outside, but there is an unmistakable sadness about him. He had been boxing for a little cash since he was sixteen but his success was always overshadowed by disaster. First, his home and property at Managua were destroyed in an earthquake in 1972. When the revolution began seven years later his brother Eduardo was killed fighting for the Sandinistas. Later his bank balance of nearly $300,000 and property were confiscated by the government and his mother and sister were turned out of Nicaragua. Fortunately he had banked a considerable amount of his ring earnings in America and he settled in Florida.

His great ambition was to become the first fighter to win four world titles, and the two thrashings he took from Pryor, only two of six defeats in eighty-four contests, sent him into a deep depression. He returned to Nicaragua to fight with the Contras against the Sandinista government but became disillusioned with both sides and returned to the United States an unhappy man. It was then he drifted into bad company and began taking cocaine. He was never really hooked and kicked the habit after some six months.

Arguello still had problems. His third marriage almost broke up and tax on ring earnings in the United States knocked a dent in another fortune. He could have ended as a tragic figure. Instead, he went back into the gym at thirty-three, determined to get completely fit. He felt so good that the urge to make history with four titles seized him again and he returned to the ring to knock out Pat Jefferson in five rounds in Alaska.

He shaped up so well in his come-back that boxing folk were predicting he might achieve an impossible dream by becoming the first fighter to win four world titles. This seemed even more possible early in 1986, two months before his thirty-fourth birthday, when he stopped Billy Costello, the former lightweight champion, in four rounds at Reno.

But fighting is a young man's game and close friends of the once super champion sensed the strain he was under in attempting to turn the clock back. Jose Sulaiman, the WBC president, advised him in the interest of his health to retire. Arguello wisely agreed. Arguello had not only fought professionally for eighteen years, won three world titles, lost two fortunes but also survived an earthquake, a revolution, three marriages and a short trip on drugs.

Don Curry

The most accomplished of the current young fighters is Don Curry, recognized as undisputed world welterweight champion by WBC, WBA and IBF. The twenty-four year old from Fort Worth, Texas is, in fact, the most complete boxer-fighter since Sugar Ray Leonard retired as undisputed champion of the same title in 1982. They call him the Cobra because of his great concentration as he meticulously weighs up opponents before suddenly striking with a venomous attack. British fans witnessed his class at Birmingham in 1985 while, performing with grace and power, he overwhelmed British champion Colin Jones in four rounds when defending the WBA welter crown. The Welshman had proved himself to be a considerable force when holding the then WBC champion Milton McCrory to a draw and a disputed losing decision in two trips to America, but Colin had no answer to the combined skill and punching talents of Curry – and was stopped in four rounds with a bad gash across the bridge of his nose.

The Texan is another of the many young black American fighters destined to win an Olympic gold medal who was frustrated, as an eighteen-year-old convinced his turn had come, when the United States boycotted the Moscow Olympics of 1980 over Afghanistan. Curry was just as big a favourite to win an Olympic title as Sugar Ray Leonard and Michael and Leon Spinks had been at Montreal four years earlier but he decided not to wait around until the Olympics at Los Angeles in 1984. He turned professional and soon ran up a string of knockout victories. When Leonard, both WBC and WBA welter champion, retired prematurely following an eye operation, Curry won the WBA version while Milton McCrory took the WBC title. Efforts were made to match the pair in order to have one champion again. By the time they met in 1985 each had established impressive undefeated records, Curry having won all his twenty-four paid contests, seventeen inside the distance and McCrory being undefeated in twenty-seven with twenty-two wins inside the distance. His only set-back was the drawn title defence against Colin Jones.

Bob Arum, the promoter, had to pay each champion $750,000 and built up interest in the fight for the undisputed title by billing it as the 'Toss-up' but Curry turned it into a massacre when fixing his eyes on the twenty-three-year-old McCrory, who stands 6 ft 1 in, and striking with such deadly accuracy and power that the affair was all over inside five minutes. Curry weighed up his opponent in the first round and carried out the destruction at the start of the second. As McCrory's guard dropped, a venomous left hook sent him flat on his back and though he rose pluckily at four, his legs and brain no longer coordinated and a right hook to the jaw finished the one-sided battle with McCrory stretched out open-mouthed and eyes rolling. Another two minutes passed before he was back on his feet after attention from the ringside doctor. It was the most deadly execution since Marvin Hagler had flattened Thomas Hearns in three rounds. The deadly finishing lifted Curry into the super champion class and on to the million dollar pay-roll. He was already planning a mega-dollar future encounter with Hagler for the middleweight championship within twelve months. While such a lucrative dream was a little premature, there was no doubt that Curry had advanced as the most talented of the younger champions and in time will be battling among the top middleweights. He has youth on his side and is seven years younger than Hagler. It will be a question of whether the great middleweight champion decides to retire or stay around long enough for yet another great pay day. But come what may, Don Curry has already been accepted as a worthy successor to the superb Sugar Ray Leonard.

A sad twist to the Curry story is that Don's older brother Bruce, who also won a world title, is now in a Nevada mental institution. Bruce, five years older than Don, won the WBC light-welterweight championship beating Leroy Haley in 1983 when reckoned to be past his best. After beating Haley again, Bruce lost the title when stopped by Billy Costello in ten rounds early in 1984. Four days after the fight he went beserk and tried to shoot his trainer Jesse Reid, firing several shots from a handgun. Poor Bruce blamed Reid for intervening during the Costello fight when the trainer was acting humanely to avoid his fighter taking further punishment. The ex-champion was arrested by the police but later committed to a mental institution.

The fight game can be both generous and cruel as the brothers Curry have discovered.

THE BEST OF BRITISH

Jack Kid Berg

Judah Bergman, one of seven children born in Whitechapel, London, in 1909 of Russian Jewish parents from Odessa, was one of the most underrated British champions. Like Ted Kid Lewis before him, his outstanding fighting ability was more appreciated in America than in Britain and his greatest performances took place in the United States. His record takes some matching, never mind beating. From the age of fourteen to thirty-eight, Jack took part in 192 bouts, winning 157, drawing nine and losing twenty-six. He was still a teenager when he crossd the Atlantic for the first time to beat some of the best featherweights and lightweights in the world, men like Tony Canzoneri, Kid Chocolate, Billy Petrolle and Mushy Callahan. He won the world junior welterweight championship by stopping Callahan, but received little credit in Britain because before the war Europe did not recognize the in-between weights which flourish today. Even before he was seventeen the Kid had fought eighteen British or European champions and before he was twenty-two he had tangled with four world title holders – Andre Routis, Tony Canzoneri, Kid Chocolate and Mushy Callahan. When Berg returned from America after six years of non-stop battling against the best around, having taken part in a hundred contests, he was considered to be past his best, although he was only twenty-five. Yet after this he won his first British title and carried on for nearly a hundred more bouts until he was thirty-eight.

Berg began boxing at the old Premierland, a famous nursery for fighters in the East End of London just before his fourteenth birthday, though he claimed he was sixteen at the time. He became affectionately known as Yiddle. He took part in sixty-two contests in the East End over ten and fifteen rounds and was only beaten three times. Then, at eighteen, he decided to try his luck in America where he told them he was twenty-one.

His American career began in Chicago. He changed his style to two-fisted all action and was given the name of the Whitechapel Whirlwind. For years his belief that attack was the best form of defence succeeded and he carried all before him. He was blessed with exceptional lungs and a slow heartbeat and reckoned that he could expand his chest by 5 inches. This partly explains why he could keep his all-action tactics going for fifteen rounds in scores of contests. His disregard for defence caught him out occasionally. After winning his first four fights in America and holding the fierce Billy Petrolle to a draw, he walked in with his chin and was stopped by Petrolle in the return, but his courage was such that having been dropped in the first and third rounds he was still fighting back when his American handler Ray Arcel tossed in the towel. After a brief visit to London, Berg was back in America thrashing Bruce Flowers (twice) and Mushy Callahan, and then was given his big chance to face Tony Canzoneri, former world featherweight champion and later to be lightweight king, in Madison Square Garden. Berg began cautiously, trying to outjab the Italian, but kept getting hit, so he changed his style and went in with both fists flying to take the decision. This made him big box office in America.

Jeff Dickson, an American promoter who presented big boxing in Paris and London, persuaded Mushy Callahan, now recognized as world junior welterweight champion in the USA, to defend that title against Berg at the Albert Hall in 1930. The British Boxing Board of Control, which had been formed a year earlier, did not recognize junior titles and had already clashed with Dickson on several accounts. I recall that Colin Symonds, an outstanding MC of his day, introduced both boxers by declaring, 'My lords, ladies and gentlemen. This is a fifteen-round contest for the junior welterweight championship of the world between . . .' He was interrupted by Lord Lonsdale, the president of the BBBC, who stood up in the front row and demanded, 'On what authority do you announce "for the junior welterweight championship of the world"?' Symonds replied respectfully, 'Because it says so in the programme, my lord'. He then repeated the same introduction and the contest went ahead. Berg had already beaten the American in a non-title bout and this time thrashed him with a display of non-stop aggression which had Callahan exhausted after ten rounds. His desperate cornerman tried everything to keep Mushy going, pouring champagne over his head, holding up smelling salts for him to inhale, and, quite ridiculously floating a cigarette lighter up and down his spine. It was, of course, to no avail. He surrendered at the end of round ten.

Berg returned to America and swept all before him, winning the next twelve bouts and defending the title nine times. He also beat the talented Kid Chocolate. This brought him another clash with Tony Canzoneri, who had become world lightweight title holder after knocking out Al Singer in the first round. Canzoneri was one of the super-lightweights, in the same league as Barney Ross, Lou Ambers, Henry Armstrong, Ike Williams, Joe Brown and Roberto Duran. This time Berg's lack of defence proved disastrous. It was all-out action for two rounds with both men throwing dozens of punches, but a devastating right to the jaw in round 3 put the Kid flat. He was out but, as always, instinctively tried to get to his feet without success. Canzoneri was still champion. That was one win each and when they met again for the title six months later Canzoneri took a fifteen-round decision.

The Londoner continued fighting but began to drop a few decisions. His world championship days were over but with his vast experience in American rings he was more than able to take care of himself back home. He caused a surprise when meeting his Jewish rival Harry Mizler from Stepney for the British lightweight title in 1934. Harry had an excellent record as an amateur. In contrast to Berg's two-fisted attack, Harry was a stylish boxer with a copybook straight left and a fair right-hand cross. He was four years younger than Berg and the experts reckoned Jack had seen his best fighting days and would not master the skilled Mizler. They had not reckoned on his experience or, in Harry's case, the lack of it.

The young champion insisted on occupying what he reckoned to be his lucky dressing room at the Albert Hall which had been allocated to Berg. As champion, Mizler claimed he had first choice. Jack would not give way, so both stripped off in the same room and Berg, more flamboyant than Mizler, began warming up, throwing punches from every angle. The confidence of the man who had fought a hundred wars in New York, Chicago and other American cities must have got to Harry, who seemed ruffled when he entered the ring and boxed below his best form. After the first two rounds in which Mizler kept his challenger away with a left jab, he could not stop Berg swarming over him and made the mistake of attempting to punch it out with a master of these tactics. Harry began to slow down and fatigue showed long before his corner retired him after ten rounds. He then had to put up with the embarrassment of having to observe the new champion celebrating in the same dressing room!

It was a bonus for Berg. He had begun fighting in the East End ten years earlier but had given up the chance to challenge for a British title, which he would most certainly have won, to go for world titles and cash in America. Now he had proved he was still the best around. He lost the British title to Jimmy Walsh at Liverpool eighteen months later. To the Kid's credit he boxed on for another decade and joined the RAF as a physical instructor during the war. He won his last three contests in 1945 before retiring.

In 1985, he was seventy-five, the Boxing Writer's Club presented him with a special trophy for outstanding services to the sport. The Kid dropped the suggestion of a tear and said it was the nicest thing that had happened to him since he had received a belt for winning the junior welterweight title fifty-five years earlier. At the time he had received no official recognition in Britain. Now more than three hundred rose to toast him, although not more than a handful had witnessed his achievement fifty-five years earlier.

Like Dempsey and Tunney, in old age Jack Kid Berg would defy any member of the BMA to say his health had suffered from his profession. He took part in nearly two hundred fights against the toughest and roughest pugilists in America in a career lasting twenty-one years.

Benny Lynch

There is a legend in Glasgow that Benny Lynch was not only the mightiest flyweight the world has seen but that, if Dempsey, Louis or Ali had bumped into Benny when he was sober, they might have ended up sprawled across Sauchiehall Street. I will go along with the first claim as fact. Benny for a few too brief years was the most outstanding flyweight I have watched. He was only 5 ft 4 in tall but after a delicate childhood developed powerful shoulders and biceps when at last escaping from a dingy tenement which did not enjoy the luxury of God's sunshine. He joined a travelling booth and began to breathe clean air and enjoy fitness for the first time.

He was taught to box as a child at St John's School by a Catholic priest. At the age of fourteen he weighed 5 stone and took part in 'midget' boxing, which was very popular in Glasgow in the twenties and thirties. At seventeen he still weighed only 7 st 6 lb but as he was only earning shillings as a labourer he decided to concentrate on the one thing he was good at – boxing. He fought regularly in Glasgow between 1931 and 1934, collecting the Scottish title from Jim Campbell. He had now arrived and his name spread beyond Scotland after he beat the Frenchman, Valentine Angleman, a former world champion, and Tut Whalley, a top flyweight.

In 1935 he held Manchester's Jackie Brown, who had taken the world flyweight title from Angleman, to a draw in a non-championship affair. This earned him a rematch for the crown at Manchester and Lynch became Britain's new boxing sensation by shattering Brown in two rounds. Jackie was reckoned to be the fastest and most skilled flyweight for many years and carried a fair punch, but he had no answer to the punching of Lynch, who had trained as never before in Sammy Wilson's gymnasium and stepped into the Belle Vue ring resembling a miniature Marciano. Brown set off at speed, but the Scot, punching like a featherweight, had him down twice in the first round. The champion attempted to go on the attack in the second round but was unable to stay the power punching of Lynch, who simply brushed him aside and sent him crashing three times with left and right hooks. Brown was brave but bewildered and had to be rescued by the referee. The title had been won in 4 minutes 42 seconds. Lynch was twenty-two; his dedication to fitness and apprenticeship in the booths had paid off.

Some 20,000 happy Scots jammed Glasgow Central Station to welcome the return of their hero. And the glum tenements in Florence Street, where he was born, became a blaze of colour with scores of Scotland's national flag garlands, flowers and many homemade messages of 'Welcome home, Champ'. After three months of celebrating he returned to the ring, winning three bouts in two weeks. But he was drinking too much with old acquaintances and began rapidly to put on weight. Never again would he attain quite the supreme physical condition he had reached when knocking out Brown. The only time he forced himslf to train with his old dedication was when defending his title.

The first warning of trouble came early in 1936 when he dropped a twelve-round decision in a non-title bout in Belfast against a good flyweight, Jim Warnock. He got down to training and won his next six bouts all inside the distance, including the defence of his titles against Pat Palmer. His next contest was the most important in his career. America had not accepted Jackie Brown or Benny as world champion. They recognized Small Montana, a brilliant boxer from the Philippines. Arthur Elvin signed the pair to meet at Wembley for the undisputed title and I rate that match as one of the most academic and skilled fifteen rounds I have ever watched. It did not have the excitement of many other bouts. There were no knock downs and the minimum of blood was spilled, but both fighters produced a display of sweet science. Benny had to be at his best to win and came in fitter than for any fight since he had knocked out Brown sixteen months earlier. Montana had an English style: he was fast with an orthodox left jab and skilled defence. Lynch, changing his tactics from the Brown fight, matched Montana in science, and for fifteen rounds we watched the near perfect match fought by two tremendous sportsmen with the referee having little to do other than score. It was a classic, with the Scot showing even more speed than the fast Filipino and taking a decision that had the appreciative onlookers giving both men a standing ovation for several minutes. After his superb victory the Scot relaxed. He was unable to discipline himself to the rigours of training in the gym and on the road, went drinking again with his old buddies, put on too many pounds and lost twice, to Len Hampston and to Jim Warnock again.

He had quarrelled with his old friend and manager Sammy Wilson before the first Warnock bout and Glasgow promoter George Dingley was quick to take over. Dingley matched him with Peter Kane, a tremendous fighter from Golborne in Lancashire. Peter was all-action and two-fisted. He had stopped Warnock and many thought he would beat Lynch if he caught the Scot on one of his now frequent off nights. But with his titles at stake the Glasgow man got down to weight and was in good condition when he faced Kane at Shawfield Park in 1937. That night the heavens opened and thousands stood for hours in the rainstorm before and during the fight. It was the last time Benny was able to make 8 stone and come in at his best. Peter was a bouncing bundle of energy who only knew one way to fight and that was going forwards. He was in trouble in the opening round as he charged into the champion, only to be dropped by the Scot's left hook. He was up quickly, too quickly in fact, and bravely carried on, but in the twelfth round fell a victim again to the champion's left hook. He did well to survive the round. He had not fully recovered when he came out for round 13 and was sent crashing. He dragged himself up at seven, only to be sent down again to be counted out. He was beaten for the first time in forty-two bouts. Kane was unlucky to have to face a Benny Lynch who only for the third time since becoming champion was in top condition. And no flyweight living could master such a phenomenon.

Early in 1938 the undisciplined Scot failed to make 8 st 6 lb for a return non-title clash with Kane at Liverpool. This time Peter held a declining Benny to a draw. When he stepped on the scales three months later to defend his title against the American Jackie Jurich, Benny, despite Turkish baths, again could not make the bantam limit and, weighing 8 st $6\frac{1}{2}$ lb, lost his titles without a punch thrown. He also had to surrender a quarter of his purse to the American, who only agreed to carry on as a non-title fight provided he received the extra cash. Lynch was too powerful for Jurich and stopped him in twelve rounds, but his world crown had been tossed on the scrap heap.

Len Harvey

Len Harvey was as unique in British boxing as was Georges Carpentier in France. Like the fabulous Frenchman, he fought at every weight, was a professional at the age of twelve, and though he finished as heavyweight champion he never scaled more than 12 st 10 lb in his career. Also like Carpentier, he was never an amateur. Though Harvey's official record consists of 133 contests, he said he had more than four hundred in and around Plymouth. He was never knocked out until his last fight against Freddie Mills when he had not boxed for three years and was just short of thirty-five. He took part in twenty-one championship fights from welter to heavyweight.

Len was born at Polhilsa, near Callington in Cornwall. The only other outstanding Cornish pugilist had been Bob Fitzsimmons, who won three world titles at different weights. Len did not achieve such honours, but he became the only British boxer to win the national middle, light-heavy and heavyweight titles. He did not come from a fighting family. When only twelve and weighing 5 st 7 lb, in order to get fights he had to cross from Cornwall into Devon and box at Plymouth for payments of five shillings. By sixteen he was travelling to London and waiting outside the old Blackfriars Ring in the hope that the promoter would be short of a fighter and looking for a substitute. He regularly fought over fifteen rounds. He was only eighteen when he faced the highly skilled welterweight champion Harry Mason for the British championship over twenty rounds. He held the champion to a draw.

He developed into a highly skilled young fighter with a perfect defence and knew how to tie up and frustrate bigger opponents inside. He learned every trick yet was scrupulously fair and a splendid sportsman, win or lose. For me, he was at his best as a middleweight between 1928 and 1933. He beat them all and was expected to be a success in America, but his cagey defensive style was not appreciated and he dropped decisions to Vince Dundee (twice) and Ben Jeby at Madison Square Garden. He had one bad night when challenging Marcel Thil for the world middleweight title at White City. Having already beaten the Frenchman, he began as favourite. The Swiss referee did not speak English and kept admonishing Len, who could not understand why and for once allowed himslf to get rattled. Thil took the decision.

One of Len's toughest fights was against Jack Casey, known as Cast-Iron Casey and the Sunderland Assassin. Harvey retained the middleweight title in a murderous battle but broke his right hand on Casey's jaw. A few months later he lost that championship on points to Jock McAvoy. Len never punched so well again but instead fell back on his great defensive skill which was to bring him the light-heavy and heavyweight titles.

Harvey was unique compared with most post-war fighters. He loved the sport more than the cash it brought him, which was little considering his marvellous record. Having lost the middleweight title to McAvoy on a close fifteen-round decision, Len won the vacant light-heavyweight championship by outpointing Eddie Phillips. He then knocked out the French middleweight Carmelo Candel in Paris, and on the way home with Jeff Dickson, who promoted in France and London, offered to fight Jack Petersen for the heavyweight title for nothing apart from training expenses! Dickson could not believe his luck and made the match at the Albert Hall in 1933. Jack was not at the top of his form that night and Harvey, by sheer ring craft and a little gamesmanship, kidded the Welshman out of the title.

Dickson was so delighted he presented Len with £100 bonus on top of £500 expenses. Can you imagine any professional fighter in the eighties being sufficiently dedicated to offer to fight for a championship for bare expenses? I am not recommending the practice because if anybody deserves the gravy in the fight game it is the fighters themselves, but Harvey's outlook is refreshing compared with the avaricious tendencies of modern sportsmen, their managers and agents, who with the aid of television demand millions and still want more.

The biggest purse Harvey earned was £5000 for defending the heavyweight title in the return fight with Petersen at White City stadium. Though Len in the fifth round received a bad cut to his eye, which had completely closed by round 8, he fought on until the twelfth when the towel came in from his corner. Despite this defeat, in his next fight he gave nearly 28 lb away to Walter Neusel, the German who had proved to be Petersen's downfall in three fights, and held Neusel to a draw.

After losing a third fight to Petersen, Harvey took over as matchmaker for Arthur Elvin at Wembley. He was already a unique champion completely managing himself. Now as matchmaker he signed himself to fight John Henry Lewis, the American holder of the world light-heavyweight championship. And what a tremendous show Harvey put on against the skilled champion. In a grandstand finish he rocked Lewis and came close to wiping out the lead John Henry had built up in the early rounds.

Jock McAvoy had become British light-heavyweight champion, stopping Eddie Phillips. Harvey met Jock and beat him at Harringay. He also won the vacant heavyweight title again when Eddie Phillips was disqualified in four rounds for a low blow. The amazing Harvey beat Larry Gains for a second time to regain the vacant Empire championship, and was matched for a return with John Henry Lewis for the world light-heavyweight crown at White City in 1939. But when the American arrived he was not allowed to box after failing to pass an eye test. The British Board then recognized a fight between Harvey and McAvoy for the vacant world 12 st 7 lb title, which Harvey won, but the Americans did not accept him as a world champion. That was in July 1939. Len did not box again for three years, having joined the RAF. He only fought once more, defending the British light-heavyweight title against Freddie Mills in 1942, but it was the ghost of the real Harvey we had known who now, aged almost thirty-five, climbed through the ropes white-faced and aware of the moment of truth. He lost his title in two rounds and announced his retirement. It was the only time he was counted out in a career of more than twenty years.

Tommy Farr

No proud holder of a British passport did more to erase the phrase 'British Horizontal Heavyweight Champion' from the American boxing lexicon than Tommy Farr. The snide phrase had come from the pen of a New York boxing writer following a series of unhappy endings to Phil Scott's battles in America. Scott's predecessors, Bombardier Billy Wells and Joe Beckett, suffered one-round annihilations at the hands of Georges Carpentier, which did not boost the export trade in British heavyweights. When Tommy Farr, an angry, hungry Welshman from Tonypandy, arrived in New York to challenge the newest sensation Joe Louis, the American writers scoffed at him, making him a 10-1 underdog. One New York columnist declared Farr had less chance against Louis than Shirley Temple. But the American writers and most British scribes were made to eat their words; they had not taken account of the toughness and guts of the man who had already won his fight against poverty. In his finest hour on 30 August 1937, Tommy Farr took on the Brown Bomber for fifteen punishing rounds, and, though he did not win the title, he won the admiration of America as well as the hearts of every man and woman in Britain.

Farr did not emerge as an overnight hero. He had sweated down the mine as a boy. At the age of twelve he was fighting in the valleys to earn a few shillings. He served the hardest apprenticeship of any British heavyweight champion, taking on all comers in the booths. His ambition was to fight in London but his early visits as a teenager brought defeats against Eddie

Steele, Eddie Phillips and Dave Carstens. He had tremendous faith in himself and was determined, despite the lack of enthusiasm from fans, not only to survive but to succeed. He moved to London, even though promoters showed no desire to give him fights or the sort of cash he felt he was entitled to. He took on Ted Broadribb as his manager. As Ted was also matchmaker for Jeff Dickson at the Albert Hall, opportunity began to knock for Farr in 1936. The ambitious Welshman received controversial decisions against the Americans Tommy Loughran and Bob Olin, both former world light-heavyweight champions, but he won little praise from British critics. This only made Farr more determined to succeed and he went on to stop Jim Wilde to become Welsh heavyweight champion. This allowed him to qualify for a crack at the British title, which was in the hands of the South African-born Ben Foord, who had beaten Jack Petersen.

Nineteen thirty-seven was a vintage year for Tommy Farr. He took the championship from Foord in a dull fight, and though he still received little credit from the boxing writers the title was his gateway to the stars. Sydney Hulls, then the top promoter, induced Max Baer, the former world heavyweight champion and a tremendous personality, to come to London to face the Welshman. The critics ridiculed the match and forecast a quick knockout for the hard-punching American playboy. They underestimated Tommy's determination and ability. Becoming British champion had boosted his already ample ego and his pride. He gave Baer a lesson in the left jab as he moved in and out, punishing the American, who in the early rounds clowned and scowled, obviously believing he had time to put the cheeky Welshman away with one big right. It never happened. That left jab split Maxie's left eye, and as the blood trickled down his face he began to show respect for Farr, who was moving with more rhythm than he had shown before. Baer, like everybody else, had underrated Farr's ring knowhow, gathered the hard way in the booths for nearly a decade.

Always a little truculent, Tommy allowed earlier resentment and bitterness to thaw and be replaced with a philosophy and wit he had picked up from old Jobey Churchill, his mentor from the hungry days in the valleys. He also revealed a new charm which made him many friends apart from the usual hangers-on who dedicate themselves exclusively to life's winners. To Farr's credit, he could recognize the spurious and thrived on the embarrassment of those who had knocked him beyond fair criticism and who were now rushing to shake his hand.

Farr's victory over Baer provided the most exciting night since Harringay was built in 1934. Never had a British heavyweight handled a top American so easily. Sydney Hulls, who in his heart had not given Farr a chance, had a new box-office king. Previously he had had to work hard at selling tickets when Tommy was fighting. But that night, as a few hundred Welsh miners who had made the journey to London nearly lifted the roof with a rendering of 'Land of My Fathers', we all realized a new Tommy Farr had been born. Hulls immediately negotiated for Walter Neusel to meet Farr. The Welshman was again in scintillating form as, moving with the speed of a middleweight, he jabbed Neusel into confusion and put him down and out in three rounds. The German had entered the ring wearing a knee support and when he failed to beat the count some accused him of quitting, but the facts are that Farr had so demoralized him that he had no stomach to fight on.

This was the period when the Nazis were preparing to take over Europe. We had seen the Olympic Games in Berlin in 1936 turned into a political jamboree for Hitler and in the same year the German leader had sent his personal congratulations to Max Schmeling who had inflicted the first defeat on Joe Louis. This night Von Ribbentrop, the German Ambassador to Britain, sat at ringside. After Neusel's defeat he immediately made for the exit.

The delighted Hulls now wanted Farr to meet Schmeling at White City. The German accepted £15,000 and Broadribb and Farr agreed to £7500, but the fight never came off because Broadribb did a better deal with Mike Jacobs for Tommy to meet Louis, who had won the world title from Braddock exactly a week before Farr knocked out Neusel. Jacobs offered Tommy £10,000. Though Broadribb had signed with Hulls, the Welshman sailed for New York in August to the annoyance of both Hulls and Schmeling.

The New York writers wrote Tommy off from the day he arrived. It was only a question of how many rounds he could last with the Brown Bomber. One? Two? Three? Or perhaps six?

The fact that they rated him so cheaply without even seeing his fight acted as a stimulus to Tommy, who was determined to make the Yankees rue their own sarcasm. And what a show the Tonypandy kid put on!

Farr was probably the only man in the Polo Grounds, New York, who believed he had any chance of beating the mighty Louis. Had he not picked up a cut eye in training a few days before, he would have stood an even better chance. His confidence was unbelievable as he walked into the champion from the first bell, despite the fact he had been called to enter the ring twenty minutes before the fight was due. Yet he had calmly sat watching a preliminary bout, an ordeal that would have unnerved most men about to face Louis. The world champion was surprised by Farr's confident aggression and still more puzzled by the Welshman's crouch. Tommy jabbed so well with his left that he soon raised a swelling under Joe's right eye and freely hit Louis about the body. All the Welshman lacked to become a world beater was a lethal right-hand punch. Louis began to settle down to hand out some pretty fierce punishment with his famed combination punches. Tommy's damaged right eye was made worse and Joe smashed some of his hardest rights against the Welshman's jaw. But the more punches Louis threw, the more Farr came back, ducking and weaving inside, always busy with his left jab and two-fisted attacks to the body. The Brown Bomber seemed determined to put a stop to the Welshman's bold bid in the seventh round when he released three smashing left hooks to Farr's chin and crossed as many times with his right, but the Welshman spat blood from his mouth, brushed aside more blood from his eye with the thumb of his glove and went back into the attack.

So it went on and on to the fifteenth and last round. The New York crowd were now cheering the brave underdog whom nobody expected to see still standing after six rounds. Tommy took a great deal of stick from the great champion. His face was badly marked yet never did he resort to a defensive role. The big difference was in their punching power and while Tommy's courage and toughness matched that of any fighter in the world, he did not have the dynamite with which to blast Joe Louis. After a magnificent stand by the challenger, Joe Louis was declared the winner and still champion. But no British fighter received more hosannas from an American fight crowd than Tommy Farr.

With hindsight, I believe Tommy made a mistake in hitching his waggon to the Mike Jacobs star. He got on well with Uncle Mike, far better than with his manager Ted Broadribb, with whom he had quarrelled after the Louis battle. Jacobs wanted to rematch Farr with Louis, but said Tommy needed a win first and thought he could easily beat Jim Braddock, whom Mike had persuaded to come out of retirement. But Braddock was a cagey boxer and as Tommy did not possess a big knockout punch, the fight was disappointing with Braddock taking the decision and Tommy's stock slumping. It would have been wiser for Farr to have gone back to Britain, defended his British title and had a few easy fights; he could then have gone back to Louis. But he stayed with Jacobs and took a return fight with Max Baer. This time Maxie gained revenge over fifteen rounds, dropping Tommy twice with tremendous rights. Jacobs still stuck by Farr and matched him with Lou Nova, but the Welshman lost another decision. His last appearance in America was against Red Burman, a moderate protégé of Jack Dempsey, but Farr dropped yet another verdict.

It was 1939 and Tommy had no option other than to return to London. He had lost all five fights in America but had finished on his feet every time. His moment of glory had been against Louis.

Though he beat Burman in a return in London and Larry Gains at Cardiff, Tommy's best days were over and he retired in 1940. He was discharged from the RAF in 1942 and for some years was a successful property dealer. Things later went wrong and Tommy, who had made and lost a fortune, returned to the ring after ten years' absence. It was a tremendous tribute to his ability that after living softly for a decade he was, at thirty-seven, able to win eleven of sixteen comeback fights. It was a pity that in this spell he suffered the only knockout defeat in his long career at the hands of Frank Bell, who would not have been able to shake the Farr of ten years earlier. Tommy showed tremendous guts in his comeback. It enabled him to straighten himself out financially. He retained the same courage he showed against Louis until his death in 1986.

Randolph Turpin

The most glorious performance by any British boxer for half a century was achieved by Randolph Turpin when he outboxed and outfought Sugar Ray Robinson at Earl's Court on 10 July 1951. Unfortunately for Turpin and Britain, it was a one-night stand; Turpin was unable to reproduce such magic. Allowing for the fact that Robinson had over-relaxed on his tour of Europe, credit cannot be taken away from the twenty-three-year-old Leamington fighter who brought off the biggest boxing upset since Jim Braddock took the heavyweight title from Max Baer in 1935. Even though the British boy lost the world title back to Robinson two months later in New York when the American no longer underestimated Turpin, we were not so far off a second British victory. If that had happened, Turpin would have joined the greatest middleweights of all time. Despite his failings, there have been few better middleweights than Randolph Turpin. Robinson endorsed this view when I chatted with him some years after his final retirement. He said, 'I never faced a fighter with more strength than Turpin. He was so strong in the clinches I thought he would break my arms.'

The Turpin achievement was mightier than the glorious victories of Tommy Farr against Max Baer, Freddie Mills winning the world title from Lesnevich, Ken Buchanan's magnificent performance to take the lightweight title from Ismael Laguna in Puerto Rico, John H. Stracey's shock defeat of Jose Napoles in Mexico City, Alan Minter's winning of the middleweight crown from Vito Antuofermo or Barry McGuigan's brilliant victory over Eusebio Pedroza for the featherweight championship.

All those victories were scored against superb fighters past their best, but Turpin, not credited with a chance of victory, outboxed and outgunned the best pound-for-pound boxer in the world to take the title by a convincing margin. It was only the great man's second defeat in eleven years and nearly 140 contests and, although, at the age of thirty-one Robinson was eight years older than his opponent, he regained the title and remained the world's top fighter for nearly another decade.

Turpin had one unusual advantage over Robinson. Sugar Ray had not come to Europe specifically to defend his crown. Jack Solomons had tempted him while he was beating moderate middleweights on the Continent. He obviously underestimated Turpin, as most British fans did, and regarded him as another moderate opponent.

Though Robinson regained the title, nothing can take away the might of the Leamington fighter's performance the first time. He was younger, stronger and fitter than Robinson. I cannot recall a more perfect physique than Turpin's muscled body that night. And the twenty-three-year old was unbelievably confident; although the bookmakers had Robinson 4-1 favourite, Turpin grinned and actually winked as the Robinson circus climbed into the ring. He went forward from the first bell, pushing a murderous left jab into the champion's face. Turpin boxed like a dream. He even controlled the much more experienced Sugar Ray in the clinches and, though rocked once or twice when the champion caught him with rights, he was never in any serious danger. Most of us at ringside had a feeling Robinson might be coasting and pacing himself before an onslaught. It never came, and when the champion's left eye was cut from an accidental clash of heads in round 7, we realized for the first time that Turpin was about to bring off a tremendous upset and become champion.

Robinson grabbed the towel at the end of the round and wiped the blood away. Though worried, he fought like a true champion, but could not swing the fight against Turpin, who was too strong to be moved. By the twelfth round every fan among the 18,000 present realized this was to be perhaps the best ever British victory; they began to sing 'For He's a Jolly Good Fellow'. So it went to the fifteenth round with Turpin strong and still in charge. The tragedy was that we never saw such a majestic performance from Turpin again. His reign as world champion lasted but sixty-four days, trouble followed trouble and the magic vanished. Every step after his greatest night was a step downwards.

But here let us concentrate on his strength and ability rather than his weaknesses, which were only revealed after his shining hour against Robinson. He had risen from obscurity by sheer boxing talent. He was the youngest of five half-caste children. His father, from British Guiana, met his white mother in the Midlands when the West Indian was demobbed after the First World War. His father, who had been gassed in the war, died when Randolph was a baby, and though his mother married again the three Turpin boys and two sisters knew all about poverty. Boxing came to the financial rescue of the boys Dick, Jackie and Randolph. A shameful rule adopted by the National Sporting Club was still in existence banning a British boy of a coloured parent fighting for the national title. It was especially shameful as Turpin's father had fought for Britain and the three brothers were to serve in the Second World War. I regularly campaigned against the unjust colour bar in British boxing and was happy to cooperate with John Lewis, the Labour MP for Bolton, in helping to get the rule erased. Dick Turpin became the first coloured British champion under BBBC rules in 1948. After he lost the middleweight title to Albert Finch, it came back to the Turpin family via Randolph.

As a child Randolph excelled at all sport. He could run faster, jump further and swim longer distances than his schoolfriends and could beat them all with his fists. His love of swimming brought about his deafness when he was trapped under water on one occasion. His apparent indifference to people was the result of this; he frequently did not hear a question put to him. Of all sport, he preferred boxing, perhaps because Dick was already established as a professional. He had been quickly spotted by George Middleton, a local shopkeeper, who also signed up Jackie and Randolph when they were young.

Randolph quickly built up a reputation with Leamington Boys Club from the age of fourteen and was greatly helped by Police Inspector Garry Gibbs. He went on to win three national junior titles and two senior ABA championships. An astonishing feat was to win a junior and senior title in the same year. With Dick in the army and Jackie in the RAF, Randolph volunteered for the Royal Navy in 1945 and became an assistant cook. He won the RN and Imperial Services titles and the ABA in 1946.

He joined Dick and Jackie as a professional in September 1946 when only eighteen and won his first fifteen bouts, all but three inside the distance. He was still in the Navy and his contests were over eight rounds. He then drew with Mark Hart, outpointed Vince Hawkins, the British middleweight champion, over eight rounds, but after his discharge was unexpectedly outpointed by Albert Finch. The big shock came in 1948 when he was dropped several times by the Frenchman Jean Stock and stopped in five rounds, but after this lapse he won his next twenty-two contests, stopping Albert Finch in five rounds to become British champion in 1950, knocking out the Dutchman Luc Van Dam to become European champion and outpointing Robinson for the world crown in 1951. Between 1949 and 1951 Randolph Turpin was Britain's most outstanding post-war champion.

Freddie Mills

To be christened Frederick Percival is not an ideal beginning for a pugilist. But it did not prevent Freddie Mills from becoming only the second English-born fighter to win the official world light-heavyweight championship, previously achieved by Bob Fitzsimmons back in 1903. Furthermore Mills did not box at school but only showed interest when he became a young milkman. His older brother Charlie had sparked his interest in the sport. Having joined a local club, he took his kid brother along as a spectator and Freddie became hooked; he and Charlie would spar for fun. He was deadly serious about becoming a fighter – not an amateur but a professional. Jack Turner, a former middleweight, was managing Albert Barton's travelling booth. Jack lived outside Bournemouth and Freddie cycled to his home and asked for a chance to become a fighter; though he did not reveal any natural skill, he possessed a great deal of strength and tons of guts. After some tuition Turner entered young Mills in a novices' competition, which he won, and soon afterwards he took part in his first professional contest, receiving just under £1 to box six rounds.

By the time he was seventeen he had won all seven professional contests and Jack Turner's brother Bob became his manager. Within another year his fame as an all-action middleweight had spread beyond Bournemouth. The Turners advised him to join the booth to get experience and Freddie took on all-comers in a tent at Chipperfield's Circus and later joined the renowned booth run by Sam McKeown. It was while with Chipperfields that he met and sparred with Gipsy Daniels, the

Welshman who in 1927 had won the British light-heavyweight title and had knocked out Max Schmeling in one round in Germany when Max was European light-heavyweight champion. The Gipsy gave Freddie his cauliflower ear.

By 1939 Mills was a good middleweight; he caused an upset in 1940 when outpointing Jock McAvoy, the British middleweight champion, in a non-title bout at Liverpool. War had been declared and Freddie was now in the RAF. Bob Turner was also about to join up, so when Ted Broadribb stepped in with an offer to buy the remaining months of a five-year agreement, Bob and Jack Turner reluctantly sold out for £200. Broadribb, who had guided Tommy Farr to the big time, was ambitious for Mills, and though he put him among the big earners, he rushed him, and at times overmatched him against heavyweights.

The Bournemouth light-heavyweight made a big impression in his first appearance at the Albert Hall, stopping Tommy Martin, the coloured Deptford heavyweight, in five rounds in September 1941. A string of contests, all against heavyweights, followed within a few weeks of each other: Freddie beat Jim Wilde, dropped a decision to Tom Reddington and gave weight and a surprise beating to Jack London. A return with Reddington ended in a nine-round victory for Freddie and a most successful one-round win against Jock McAvoy, which was a final eliminator for the British light-heavyweight championship, earned Mills a challenge against Len Harvey in June 1942.

Harvey also held the British heavyweight championship but was almost thirty-five and had not boxed for three years, having become an officer in the RAF. It was the match that made Freddie Mills famous. It took place on a Saturday afternoon at the Tottenham Hotspur ground and Mills was paid £1000, which he considered to be a fortune. Freddie, twelve years younger than Harvey, used his youth and strength from the first bell. It was all over in the second round. Len, looking old and without the strength of his peak years, was caught several times and pushed to the ropes. Yet another left hook sent him out of the ring. He rose but was too shaken to climb back before the count of ten.

Although Len was heavyweight champion, the title was not at stake. Broadribb was anxious for Mills to win this crown and in 1944 Freddie faced Jack London for this vacant championship at Manchester. If it had been another ten-rounder Freddie would have won again, but London, with more than 30 lb weight advantage, finished stronger in the closing rounds and took the decision and title.

In 1945 the RAF shipped Mills overseas to India where he served for twelve months. With the war in Europe over, Jack Solomons took over as Britain's top promoter by matching London with Bruce Woodcock for the heavyweight title at the Tottenham Hotspur ground, and a new era resulted when Bruce knocked out the old champion in six rounds. Solomons, anxious to promote a match between Woodcock and Mills as soon as Freddie came home from India, contacted Broadribb. Solomons had arranged a deal with the Greyhound Racing Association for the exclusive use of Harringay. Broadribb was a shrewd operator. While agreeing to a meeting between Freddie and Woodcock, he was also negotiating for a future world light-heavyweight title fight against Gus Lesnevich, the American champion.

Everybody was anxious to cash in on the coming post-war boom in boxing, and a great deal of wheeling and dealing went on which brought in the cash but was not in the best physical interest of either boxer. Once Broadribb knew Mills's discharge date, he agreed for him to meet Woodcock in a non-title twelve rounder at Harringay in June 1946. He then moved in on Lesnevich and Solomons persuaded the American to come to Harringay and defend the championship on 14 May. Meanwhile Tom Hurst, the manager of Woodcock, was also chasing the cash and agreed that Woodcock should face the tough American heavyweight Tami Mauriello at Madison Square Garden on 13 May 1946.

Everybody earned a great deal of cash. Solomons charged twenty guineas for ringside seats and had a £50,000 sellout for Mills and Lesnevich and another full house for the Woodcock bout three weeks later. I wrote at the time that Jack Solomons, Ted Broadribb and Tom Hurst were not protecting their young prospects. Woodcock was knocked out in five rounds by Mauriello. It was his first defeat. Mills, too brave for his own good, was even more heavily punished by Lesnevich after putting up a tremendous stand for ten rounds. Thus our two best post-war prospects were beaten by far more experienced Americans. And three weeks after they were flattened, they were put in against each other for a punishing twelve rounds.

It is a tribute to the courage and strength of Mills that, after being disgracefully mismatched against Joe Baksi, a leading American heavyweight, and being stopped in six rounds, he survived to win the world light-heavyweight title, outpointing a fading Lesnevich two years after taking such a terrible hammering in their first meeting. But still Ted Broadribb could not resist chasing the impossible dream and in 1949 Freddie signed for another clash with Woodcock, this time with the heavyweight crown at stake. Gallant Freddie had another go but the old snap had long been knocked out of him. He was counted out in the fourteenth round. In little over three years Freddie Mills, as brave a fighter as I have seen, had his will to win crushed. After being knocked out in ten rounds by the American Joey Maxim to lose the world championship, Broadribb announced his retirement. Freddie Mills was a splendid light-heavyweight. His heart was bigger than his frame.

Howard Winstone

If it had not been for an accident in a toy factory at Merthyr soon after his fifteenth birthday, Howard Winstone might have become Britain's most renowned champion, perhaps even greater than those three patriarchs of Welsh boxing – Jim Driscoll, Freddy Welsh and Jimmy Wilde. Howard was earning less than £3.50 a week operating a machine manufacturing metal blackboards and easels when his right hand was crushed. The tops of three fingers were amputated, which meant he would never carry a knockout punch in his right hand. Despite this disability, he won the British European and world featherweight titles and two Lonsdale Belts. The world title came in the twilight of his career after three murderous losing battles against the magnificent Mexican Vicente Saldivar, contests which took their toll on both champions.

Winstone was one of the most skilled boxers Britain produced, even more stylish than Nel Tarleton, the first champion to win outright two Lonsdale Belts. Perhaps the mixture of Welsh, Irish, English and Jewish blood flowing through his veins was the recipe for the perfect fighting cocktail. Though born in Wales, only his father's mother was Welsh. His mother's father came from Ireland and her mother was Jewish. Howard's father and grandfather were English costermongers. They peddled scrap with an old horse and cart in the Merthyr valley, rather like Steptoe and Son. Such was the poverty in the valley that Howard's father joined the army as a regular and was wounded with the Welsh Regiment on D-Day. He died before seeing his son box as a professional.

It was his father who started Howard's interest in fighting when he bought a pair of boxing gloves and taught him a few tricks in the kitchen. Howard was ten at the time. Such was his enthusiasm and progress that at eleven he was sparring and training in the New Drill Hall, Georgetown. By fifteen he had won three Welsh schoolboy championships and a British senior title. Then came the accident which put him out of boxing and work for more than a year and forced him on the dole. He was going steady with Benita and they had already decided to get married. The wedding took place when Benita was sixteen and Howard seventeen, thanks to the help of his father, who lent them £1900 of his savings to buy a two-room house. Howard was still mad on boxing and by 1956 had met Eddie Thomas, the former British and European welterweight champion, who had a gym in an old billiard hall at Penydarren less than a hundred yards from where Winston was born.

Eddie, who had a good left jab himself, helped to develop Howard's skill and, more important, convinced him he could become a champion without a right-hand punch, by dominating with his left. While training with Thomas, Winstone won all thirty-three amateur contests over eighteen months. He boxed for Wales five times and won ABA and Empire Games bantamweight championships. He was only nineteen.

By now he was working in a brewery but, having started a family, money was short and he desperately wanted to turn professional. However, Eddie wisely held him back, wanting to make sure the handicapped right hand would not prove disastrous if he joined the tougher ranks of the professionals. Howard was completely dedicated and Eddie gave him the go-ahead a few months before he was twenty. He felt like a millionaire when he picked up £60 for his first professional contest and outpointed Bill Graydon over six rounds at Wembley. Within two years he had become British featherweight champion, stopping Terry Spinks in ten rounds. He remained undefeated in thirty-four bouts until he got tagged by Leroy Jeffrey, a hard-hitting American, in a two-round shock defeat at Leeds in 1962. He was down twice and saved from a knockout only by the intervention of the referee. The cynics declared he had a glass chin and wrote him off, but they could not have been more wrong. Winstone proved his chin matched his tremendous courage during the next six busy years, defending the British title six times, winning the European championship and defending it without defeat seven times and winning the WBC crown at his fourth attempt.

His three encounters with Saldivar were classics, combining skill, courage and incredible stamina. The first bid for the title took place at Earl's Court in 1965 and the Welshman performed like a matador, tormenting and frustrating the bull-like Mexican, moulded like a welterweight from the waist up, as he jabbed the perfect left into his bruised face for six rounds. Yet Saldivar, who boxed four-minute rounds in training, had built up a tremendous reserve of stamina. He could turn on a devastating two-fisted attack to the body and seemed geared to put on pressure for the last thirty seconds of every round. If only Winstone's right fist had the power to slow down this pocket Marciano! As it was, the Mexican's ability to appear fresh and strong in the closing rounds won him a narrow decision.

When they met again at Ninian Park, Cardiff, nearly two years later it was even closer. This time many experts joined Eddie Thomas and Winstone in their opinion they had been robbed when the referee decided the Mexican had won by half a point. For ten rounds Winstone again boxed with style as his efficient left found its target. However, from the seventh round the little Mexican was scoring with more damaging blows at infighting. Yet after ten rounds he must have realized his title was in danger because he came charging out in the eleventh; only sheer guts kept the Welshman going as he was punished to body and head. The fourteenth round was torturous for Howard. The Mexican bull rushed him into a neutral corner and staggered him with a long swinging left. Then it was nonstop: blow after blow to head and body had the Welshman as limp as a rag doll. His lips were bloodied and swollen and there was a gash under his left eye, and when he slumped down the ropes few of us present thought his rubbery legs could raise his sore body. But he dragged himself up at eight and with outstanding valour stayed on his feet till the end of the round, defying Saldivar to put him down again before the final bell. It was touch and go, almost a draw, but I have always believed a referee must find a winner after twelve or fifteen rounds, and I did not dispute

Wally Thom's decision. But I doubt if any other country in the world would have given the verdict to the foreigner. Saldivar agreed with those sentiments.

The third clash took place at Mexico City four months later. Once again Winstone's left jab dominated the fight for half a dozen rounds but he did not have the ammunition to sap the Mexican of his reserve supply of energy. So, once again, Saldivar released his late blitz and Winstone, cut and bruised, was punched round the ring in round 12 and put down for eight. He rose to continue, but Eddie Thomas threw in the towel. This upset Winstone, who wanted to go down fighting. Then came a most dramatic and unexpected announcement from the ring. Saldivar, after seven defences, was to give it all up at twenty-four. He had made this decision halfway through the contest!

His dramatic conclusion was perhaps the most intelligent statement any champion ever made. 'We have taken too much out of each other in three battles. I feel it is time for me to quit.' It brought a light back into Winstone's sad eyes. Surely the only featherweight in the world who could frustrate his life's ambition to win a world title was Saldivar. So perhaps he should try yet again before he also retired. He was correct. The Mexican retired and three months later in London Winstone stopped the Japanese Mitsunori Seki, who had twice been beaten by Saldivar, with a cut eye in nine rounds, to win the WBC title.

Winstone then made the mistake of not quitting as champion. He was fading fast, as was proved when he was floored by Jimmy Anderson in his next bout, a non-title affair which he won on points. He lost the crown after six months in his first defence against the Cuban Jose Legra whom he had once beaten. This fight at Porthcawl ended in five rounds, but it was virtually over in the first when Legra swung a looping right that landed above Winstone's left eye and sent him crashing. He was up at two but his eye had already closed and he was knocked down again. He never gave up but had no chance with one eye completely closed. When Harry Gibbs wisely led the brave Winstone back to his corner in the fifth round, he was also leading him into permanent retirement. His purse of £12,000 was the most he had earned. Winstone's record was magnificent. He lost only six of sixty-seven contests. He had never taken the full count and no opponent from Europe or Britain ever beat him.

To emphasize that Saldivar belonged with the super-featherweights such as Sandy Saddler and Willie Pep, after eighteen months' retirement he returned to win the title again, beating Johnny Famechon, who had outscored Legra. He lost the crown to the Japanese Kuniaki Shibata in thirteen rounds in 1970, won his only contest against Frankie Crawford in 1971 and unwisely, after more than two years out of action, attempted to win the title a third time but was beaten in four rounds by Eder Jofre in Brazil.

Ken Buchanan

After Benny Lynch, Ken Buchanan was Scotland's outstanding champion. Lynch may have reigned for a decade but on paper Ken's record is the more impressive. Yet though he boxed professionally for eighteen years, a chip on the shoulder and an impulsive temperament made him his own worst enemy. Buchanan quarrelled with manager Eddie Thomas and made badly timed decisions to quit boxing which damaged his career.

Yet at his peak there had been no finer British lightweight than Buchanan since the days of Freddy Welsh. He was one of a handful of British fighters to win a world title on hostile territory and defend it abroad. His reign as world champion was less than two years but he was unlucky to coincide with the arrival of a super young fighter from Panama, Roberto Duran, who cut Buchanan's time at the top considerably. By comparison Jim Watt, though a skilful boxer, was even more skilfully steered to the world title; he did not have to face Duran, who had moved to a higher weight division. With the lightweight cupboard comparatively bare, Watt won the vacant title in Glasgow, defended it there four times, lost it at Wembley and then retired. It was a different ballgame.

Buchanan was not born into a fighting family but was a born fighter. His aunt bought him a pair of boxing gloves when he was eight. His father Tom promised the lad he would make him a member of the Sparta Club in Edinburgh and Ken had his first contest at the age of nine, weighing but 3 st 2 lb. His progress was tremendous and he was ABA featherweight champion before the age of twenty. He turned professional in

1965, making his debut at the National Sporting Club and winning the British crown from Maurice Cullen there three years later.

It was impressive to be boxing under chandeliers at dinner clubs but he was not collecting as much as he thought he was worth. Twenty-five of his first thirty-three professional fights took place in clubs. His manager, Eddie Thomas, was working with Jack Solomons, who was warring with the combination of Jarvis Astaire, Harry Levene, Mickey Duff, Terry Lawless and later Mike Barrett. The Scot appealed to the British Boxing Board to end his contract with Thomas when it still had two and a half years to run. When the Board upheld the contract, Ken impetuously announced his retirement and returned his Lonsdale Belt. He was only twenty-four and was undefeated in thirty-three professional bouts. He clearly felt strongly when he declared he would never box again. He intended resuming his trade as a carpenter, but a month later had second thoughts, patched up his quarrel with Eddie and agreed to a warm-up fight for Solomons before challenging for the vacant European title in Madrid where he lost a disputed decision to Miguel Velasquez. He then retained his British crown, knocking out Brian Hudson at Wembley, but it was a poor house. Ken was to be bigger box office in New York than in London.

His luck changed a few months later. Bill Daly, a big-time American fight manager in the States, had moved to Puerto Rico and was influential there. He contacted Jack Solomons and suggested a possible meeting at San Juan for Buchanan against Ismael Laguna of Panama for the WBC title. Eddie Thomas and Ken were all for it, and though Laguna began 5–2 favourite Buchanan fought a tremendous battle. After falling behind with two badly cut eyes, he rallied in the closing rounds in a temperature of 100 degrees to snatch a split decision and the world title.

Ironically, the WBC did not recognize the Scot as champion because Laguna had declined to meet Mando Ramos from whom he had won the championship. As the British Boxing Board is affiliated to the WBC, Ken was not recognized in Britain – after achieving what no other Briton had done since Ted Kid Lewis fifty-five years earlier, winning a world title abroad. Ken was now at his peak, thrashing Donato Paduano in

Madison Square Garden, defending the title against Ruben Navarro, getting recognition from the WBC as champion and then beating Laguna again in New York.

But he and Thomas rowed again over terms. Their contract was up. Eddie refused to agree to the new terms Ken was demanding and announced in the press he was through with Buchanan. An angry Ken threatened to quit boxing once more but, after winning bouts in London and Johannesburg, he signed to defend the world crown against Duran at Madison Square Garden where he was beaten in a brawling eleven rounds. Ken carried on fighting without Thomas, winning all thirteen bouts. He had lost some of his old fire and ambition but he beat Jim Watt to regain the British title he had relinquished, winning a Lonsdale Belt outright in the process. He then went to Sardinia and won the European championship, stopping Antoni Puddu in six rounds, and defended it stopping Leonardo Tavarez in Paris. He went globe-trotting again to Tokyo to bid for the world crown against the Japanese holder Ishimatsu Suzuki. Nearly five years had passed since he had first won the title in San Juan and although it was yet another brave performance from Ken, who battled on with a cut eye, he had passed his peak and narrowly lost the decision.

Undaunted, he went into the enemy camp once more to defend the European title in Sardinia against Giancarlo Usai a local boy. He was struggling in the early rounds but staged another of his gutsy rallies, forcing the referee to stop the fight in his favour. The locals rioted, tossing bottles and cans into the ring. He suffered blurred vision in this bout and was aware that some of the old sparkle was missing. He was thirty and had been boxing, boy and man, for twenty-two years. He had grossed around £250,000 – most of it from a few American fights – and had kept sufficient to buy a small hotel. He was still champion of Europe. He announced his retirement in 1975. This should have been the perfect end to the Buchanan story but it was not to be. Four years later Ken returned to the ring strictly for the cash. In his absence Jim Watt had won the British, European and world titles and collected a fortune without having to do it the hard way. Ken won two fights in Denmark, collected new supporters and made a spirited bid to win the European title again from Irishman Charlie Nash in Copenhagen. Though many Danish fans thought he had won, he had taken a great deal of punishment and lost the decision. It was to be Ken Buchanan's last championship fight.

BOOK TWO

THE BAD

The author

Above left: Jack 'Kid' Berg, one of Britain's greatest fighters. In a career of twenty-one years, he took part in nearly 200 contests, challenging the toughest American champions. Winner of the world junior welterweight title, he had fought eighteen British and European champions before he was seventeen and four world champions at twenty-one

Above right: One of Britain's finest champions, Len Harvey won the middle, light-heavy and heavyweight titles. He is seen here in his later years sitting beneath a portrait of himself when he was champion

Below: 'Last one up is a cissy!' Playboy Max Baer teases Primo Carnera after they have tripped over each other during their heavyweight championship clash in 1934. Baer took the title from the Italian giant in eleven rounds, having floored him in every round

Above left: Toughest of all British heavyweights, Tommy Farr defies Joe Louis to drop him in their fifteen rounds slam at Yankee Stadium, New York in 1937. Though he failed to take the heavyweight crown this was the Welshman's finest hour

Above right: Henry Armstrong wins the first of three world crowns by punishing Petey Sarron to become featherweight champion in 1937

Below left: Freddie Mills, a strong light-heavyweight who was thrown in against too many heavyweights

Below right: Back from hell — Henry Armstrong, the great triple champion, having sunk to the depths after a trip to Skid Row, pulls himself together to become a Baptist Minister

The greatest pound for pound fighter of all time, in the opinion of the author: Sugar Ray Robinson wins the middleweight crown in 1951 stopping Jake La Motta, the 'Raging Bull', in thirteen rounds

Even as a balding thirty-seven-year-old, the old Brown Bomber, when making a come-back, was still too good for Lee Savold who had stopped Bruce Woodcock in four rounds in London. Lee was battered to defeat in six rounds by Louis

The Duke of Edinburgh makes a rare appearance inside a boxing ring to greet Don Cockell before facing Jim Slade, reckoned to be an 'easy' opponent, in 1951. But Prince Philip also greeted the black New Yorker who bowed with delight and was so inspired that he caused a big upset, knocking out Cockell in four rounds

Archie Moore drops Rocky Marciano in the first round of a heavyweight championship clash before Rocky recovered to knockout Archie in round 9

Rocky Marciano, the hardest hitter since Dempsey. Marciano twists 'Jersey Joe' Walcott's face like a rubber mask when knocking out Jersey Joe to become heavyweight champion at Philadelphia, 1952

Baer still a playboy: Baer returns to London for Harringay's last night for the parade of the champions who fought there. Maxie shapes up to Rinty Monaghan, the former world flyweight champion

Farewell to Harringay. After twenty-two years as Britain's greatest boxing arena, Harringay is to become a warehouse. So in October 1958 Jack Solomons stages a Night to Remember, bringing together a few of the famous names who had fought there. *Front row:* Joe Erskine, Phil Edwards, Terry Downes, Henry Armstrong, Gus Lesnevich, Sammy McCarthy, Peter Waterman, Johnny Williams. *Second row:* Randolph Turpin, Dave Crowley, Harry Mizler (hidden), Ernie Roderick, Peter Kane, Rinty Monaghan, Ronnie Clayton, Jack Solomons, Johnny Best junior, Eric Boon, Len Harvey, Don Cockell. *Back row:* Jack Petersen, Bruce Woodcock, Max Baer, Arthur Danahar (hidden), Tommy Farr and Eddie Phillips (both hidden)

Sonny Liston stands triumphant as the new heavyweight king after flattening Floyd Patterson in the first round at Chicago in 1962. Liston repeated the one-round treatment of Patterson at Las Vegas in 1963

Monopoly

Monopoly in any walk of life must be bad. It aims to stifle opposition, eliminate competition and become omnipotent. We all know that power corrupts. Human nature is such that the norm in big business is to grow and grow. Monopoly is becoming accepted as inevitable in an age when the tycoons are geared to bigger and bigger takeovers.

Boxing is no exception and television, with its continual ratings war, is just as anxious to monopolize it as any promoter. While it is not in the best interests of any sport to have one man dictating, making and breaking the rules, it is inevitable that in boxing there will always be one man with the ambition to become the Number One promoter.

In the bare-knuckle days the prize money was put up by wealthy backers. Promoters, as such, did not exist until a group of businessmen who formed the Olympic Club staged the Sullivan–Corbett heavyweight championship in New Orleans in 1892. Gloves were used and a purse of $25,000 was put up with another $20,000 in stake money. After this era America produced famous promoters like James J. Coffroth and Tom Carey but the most successful was Tex Rickard. Rickard was the first promoter to attract a million-dollar gate and he only did this with a monopoly of Jack Dempsey's services. Rickard was a real promoter who gambled with his own cash. He was a showman in the Barnum mould. For the first million-dollar gate, between Demsey and Georges Carpentier, he took over a swamp area, known as Boyle's Thirty Acres, in Jersey City and constructed a stadium for one fight only. It was 1921 and the

First World War was still in the minds of Americans. A great publicist, Rickard built up the image of Carpentier as a war hero, while Dempsey, who had not joined the US services, received rough treatment in the newspapers. More than 80,000 fans turned up, with ringsiders paying a hitherto unheard of $50 each for a seat. The receipts totalled just under $1,800,000. Dempsey flattened the smaller Carpentier in four rounds, and with exclusive use of the champion, Rickard promoted five separate contests, each exceeding one-million dollars. Rickard also inspired the building of Madison Square Garden on Eighth Avenue in 1925, promoting the Paul Berlenbach–Jack Delaney world light-heavyweight championship. It became known as the House that Tex Built and was the third venue to be called Madison Square Garden.

Rickard was a gambler from Montana who rode tall in the saddle and played poker for thousands of dollars. He was regarded as a straight shooter. He had promoted the Joe Gans–Battling Nelson epic at Goldfield, Nevada, and the Johnson–Jeffries affair at Reno, Nevada, refereeing the latter contest himself. He gave Dempsey the chance to win the heavyweight title from Jess Willard in Toledo, Ohio. When Tex died in 1930 at the age of sixty, his successor Mike Jacobs, a ticket tout when Rickard was promoting, had learned the lesson of monopoly. 'Uncle Mike' ran Madison Square Garden and his Twentieth Century Club monopolized the heavyweight championship though it had lost some of its huge box-office appeal with the retirement of Dempsey and Tunney.

Schmeling, Sharkey, Carnera, Baer and Braddock followed as champion, but none of them could draw a million-dollar gate. It took Joe Louis in his second appearance in New York against the dethroned Baer in 1935 to bring back the million dollars, achieved for the first time in a non-title contest. Mike Jacobs virtually took over Louis for the rest of his fighting life. At the end of the war Jacobs controlled a $16-million-a-year empire and the destiny of every worthwhile champion. In 1946 he staged the second Louis–Conn championship with the first $100 ringside seats. His reign ended suddenly when he suffered a stroke in 1947.

When Jacobs died six years later, Jim Norris, a wealthy businessman and boss of Chicago Stadium, took over and formed the International Boxing Club. Unfortunately for American boxing, Norris was not appalled by the infiltration of hoodlums like Frankie Carbo and allowed the gangster's grip to grow. In the end Washington's attention was drawn to the IBC and in 1957 Norris and some fellow directors were found guilty of monopolistic practices and ordered to disband. Eventually Carbo was indicted and jailed and boxing in the United States had its biggest clean-up. With the collapse of the IBC, Cus D'Amato, an eccentric but honest fight manager, set out to change the scene. Cus, a sworn enemy of the IBC, refused to do business with anyone who had been remotely connected with it. Rocky Marciano, controlled by Al Weill, matchmaker of Madison Square Garden, and an associate of Norris, had retired. Floyd Patterson, managed by D'Amato, won the vacant title by knocking out Archie Moore. As long as Patterson remained champion, D'Amato held the reins. Cus was obsessed with beating old enemies and became so suspicious that he chose his own promoters without realizing he was now joining the dictators. He remained a power for six years, handpicking Patterson's challengers, but eventually was forced by public opinion to accept Sonny Liston, permanently barred by New York State because of hoodlum connections, as an opponent. Liston twice destroyed Floyd in less than one round, in Chicago and Las Vegas, but his anticipated reign of terror was cut short seven months later by the arrival from Louisville, Kentucky, of the remarkable young Cassius Marcellus Clay II.

America's two most successful promoters since Mike Jacobs have been Bob Arum and Don King but, unlike Jacobs and Rickard, they have been able to gamble with television money. They are complete opposites with only two things in common: they each like money and each dislikes the other. Arum was first on the boxing scene in the early seventies. Slightly built, he comes from a Jewish family in Brooklyn. On leaving Harvard Law School with an honours degree in 1956, he worked for the US Attorney General. Ten years later he was invited to represent legally the promoters of the Ali–Chuvalo heavyweight championship in Toronto. By 1977 as chairman of Top Rank he had promoted thirteen world title fights for television. His fascination with the fight game had started in 1962 when he was sent to Chicago by the US Government's

Internal Revenue Service to investigate tax negotiations for the first Liston–Patterson championship. He also played a major role in organizing Ali's contracts to fight Henry Cooper in London and Karl Mildenberger in Frankfurt and many other Ali bouts.

Then came the challenge from Don King, a black extrovert, whose ostentatious style of dressing with diamond rings and candyfloss hairstyle make Liberace appear to be in perpetual mourning. King, who operated the numbers game in Cleveland, killed a man he said was cheating him. He was charged with murder, which was later reduced to manslaughter, and served four years in jail. He was next heard of in boxing when he secured a match for heavyweight Earnie Shavers in Madison Square Garden.

King shook the boxing world when he set up the meeting between Ali and George Foreman, then the champion, in Zaîre in 1974. Each fighter received more than $5 million. Ali regained the title and King promoted his defences against several challengers, including Joe Bugner in Kuala Lumpur. Then followed a strange marriage when King and Arum put together the third Ali–Frazier fight announced as the 'Thrilla in Manila', but they had a difference of opinion over a little thing called money and have been warring ever since. King took charge of Larry Holmes, Ali's sparring partner in Zaîre, and when Holmes became champion King was able to control all important heavyweight championships.

King is a born survivor. Having overcome his term in prison, he survived a scandal described as boxing's Watergate in 1977. He thought up an idea of a US championship tournament for television to discover new champions. ABC Television sponsored it to a tune of $1.5 million but pulled out later, and the tournament was cancelled. This did not stop King from continuing to put on big fights for television and he still rivals Arum for the title of Number One.

What of monopoly in British boxing? I suppose the worst days existed when the old National Sporting Club was founded in 1891. For many years it was the home of boxing, but althought it was set up by a bunch of Corinthians with Lord Lonsdale as its president, it ruled and dictated boxing as never before or since. The Club revised the Queensberry Rules, introduced the famous Lonsdale Belts and set a monopoly on all championships by refusing to recognize a champion defending his title unless the contest took place in the club's headquarters in Covent Garden. The worst thing the Club did was to introduce the colour bar because Jack Johnson had broken his promise to fulfil an engagement after becoming world champion. This rule, which prevented any British boxer with a coloured parent from fighting for a national championship, continued until after the last war.

Several promoters rebelled against the NSC stranglehold. Most prominent was Charles B. Cochran, the stage entrepreneur. He staged bouts involving Carpentier, Beckett, Bombardier Billy Wells, Jimmy Wilde, Mickey Walker, Tommy Milligan and many more. When the old NSC went into liquidation in the late twenties, Jeff Dickson, an American living in Paris, ran the big promotions at London's Albert Hall and White City. He brought the giant Carnera from Paris to box America's Young Stribling and remained top boxing man in Britain for some years. There were many other promoters around. Johnny Best staged some tremendous shows at Liverpool Stadium and on Liverpool Football Club ground. Regular promotions took place at Belle Vue, Manchester, and in Newcastle and Glasgow and all round Britain in local swimming baths and corn exchanges. Arthur Elvin, who owned Wembley Stadium and the Empire Pool, promoted high-class tournaments in the thirties with Len Harvey and Sydney Hulls as matchmakers. Later Hulls moved to promote big shows for the Greyhound Racing Association at Harringay and White City. Plenty of other regular shows were held in London at Blackfriars Ring, Premierland, Devonshire Club and dozens of small halls, with the new National Sporting Club promoting regularly under Jack Harding at the Empress Hall, Earl's Court. There was no monopoly and the sport was healthy with more than 3000 registered professional boxers.

Jack Solomons began to move into the West End from the East End, thanks to the success of Eric Boon, a lethal-punching young lightweight from Chatteris. As manager, Solomons gave Sydney Hulls exclusive rights over Boon after he had won the title, knocking out Dave Crowley when only eighteen. The war intervened. Hulls soon quit boxing, and although several promoters came and went, Solomons moved in and was ready to take over as Number One by 1945, promoting the Jack London–Bruce Woodcock heavyweight championship at Tottenham Hotspur ground. With Woodcock winning the heavyweight title and Freddie Mills the light-heavyweight crown from Len Harvey, Jack had two big names to promote. He took over at Harringay and White City, working with the GRA. In 1946 he was able to charge twenty guineas for tickets for Mills *v.* Lesnevich and Woodcock *v.* Mills and established himself as Mr Boxing. He began tie-ups first with Mike Jacobs and then with Jim Norris in New York and Gilbert Benaim in Paris. He was a good promoter with some of Rickard's flair for showmanship and publicity. He had created a monopoly, pulling all the strings for the puppets to obey.

Working as his manager was Sam Burns, as shrewd an operator as I ever met. Son of Sid Burns, a good middleweight, Sam started as a kid in Fleet Street at the *Sporting Life*. Far more brilliant with figures than words, he became a wizard in racing and betting and, realizing he would never become rich in Fleet Street, moved from the *Life* at the same time as the boxing writer Stanley Longstaff. Together they helped an unnamed wealthy woman to promote the Jack Petersen–Jock McAvoy heavyweight championship at Earl's Court in 1936. The promotion flopped financially and the name of the lady remained anonymous. Burns had an uncanny knack of perfect timing to know when to get on his bike. He worked for John Harding at the NSC, John Muldoon, who staged the Harvey–Mills fight, Jack Cappell and Solomons. As Solomons also ran a bookmaking business, Sam was a perfect partner and together they were financially successful, signing up some of the best amateurs to be managed by Burns. Jack and Sam were the very best of friends.

Jack was happy to be King Solomons in his gymnasium opposite the Windmill Theatre. He held daily court in a tiny office. The boxing writers and top managers like Jim Wicks and Harry Levene were welcome in the inner sanctum. The rest had to wait in the gym.

Solomons would not accept that kings are deposed, empires fall and life goes on. He wanted to remain Number One and was not impressed by the emergence of a younger man who had returned from America and took a big interest in boxing. I recall Burns saying to Solomons one day, 'Jarvis Astaire is still waiting to see you' and was given the quick reply, 'Let him wait!' This turned out to be one of Jack's biggest mistakes for, although at this stage Astaire was only a fight manager who looked after Billy Thompson, the lightweight champion, and Peter Waterman, the welter champion, he was ambitious and with bright ideas on the future of boxing and television. Had Solomons worked with Astaire, he would probably have remained Number One for perhaps another decade because Jarvis has always been prepared to work at a distance.

It was a start of a bitter war. Mickey Duff, a former boxer, was becoming a successful matchmaker but never hit it off with Solomons. Burns and Solomons fell out. Soon there was a combination of Astaire, Duff, Burns and Levene opposing Solomons, with Levene as the promoter. To add to Solomons's problems, he lost Harringay, the perfect boxing arena, when the GRA sold it. Levene moved into Wembley Arena. The decline and fall of the Solomons empire had begun. Astaire and Duff organized the Anglo-American Club at the Dorchester Hotel in Park Lane. This became a successful dinner-jacketed wine, dine-and-watch boxing set-up. Solomons tried his luck at Wembley but lost money and started the World Sporting Club at Grosvenor House, also in Park Lane, but he had lost the initiative and became the promoter who always finished second.

Between 1945 and 1958 Solomons had been a terrific promoter. He was brash and egotistical. Boxing was fun while Jolly Jack was wisecracking his way to the top, but he could not accept competition, and instead of fighting back he became obsessed with a war of attrition. He kept screaming monopoly, forgetting he had enjoyed such a state for more than a decade. Eventually the BBBC ordered a probe by its Southern Area Council of which Solomons was the chairman, but nothing was proved. It was a pity Solomons allowed his bitterness to eat into him. He took it to the grave.

A new promoter, Mike Barrett, had arrived and struck up a partnership with Mickey Duff. Barrett, not as brash as the average promoter, soon settled in with Duff to run many successful tournaments. However, it is Jarvis Astaire who has had the biggest influence on British boxing since the fall of Solomons. He was born in the East End where his family ran a hat manufacturing business. He attended a boarding school at Westcliff-on-Sea and Kilburn Grammar School. After a spell in America he opened a men's wear business but was more interested in property development. He had always been a sports fan with a special liking for boxing. Among his many successful business ventures was the purchasing of Hurst Park racecourse. Realizing the boom that bookmakers would enjoy with the Betting and Gaming Act about to make betting legal in shops, he formed the Hurst Park Syndicate, selling the old racecourse to builders. With Sam Burns and Terry Downes he began to construct a betting-shop empire. All three made fortunes. William Hill later took over their shops and Burns became managing director. Astaire also launched Viewsport, a successful company which shows big fights and other sport live in cinemas throughout the country.

After Solomons there was little doubt that big boxing promotions aided by lucrative BBC contracts were in the hands of an exclusive few. Mike Barrett was progressing; Mickey Duff turned his attention to promoting in America and eventually moved to the United States, returning for the promotions at Wembley or wherever the big fights were held. The first real challenge came unexpectedly when a young man, Frank Warren, decided he would enjoy the hassle of the fight game. He made a false start by launching unlicensed shows using veteran boxers and without any control. These tournaments were no serious challenge to the promoters of Wembley and Albert Hall tournaments but Warren later became a licensed promoter and, though lacking arenas with the capacity of those hired by his rivals, began to become a tough competitor with high financial bids, which enabled him to promote British, European and even world title fights.

Warren's challenge was financially backed by television. ITV were struggling to compete with the BBC who had exclusive contracts for the Wembley and Albert Hall shows. ITV were happy to deal with Warren if he could deliver big fights or big names. That is where Joe Bugner came in. He was glad to return to Britain and fight for Warren and ITV did business. Bugner caused a momentary stir on television but soon faded.

He fell out with Warren and returned to America, but the new promoter had established himself as a contender in the promotion stakes. Another boxing war began.

The Build-Up

One of the most controversial subjects in professional boxing is the build-up. A reasonable build-up is essential to protect a novice. It is a necessary evil but in extreme cases it can become an abuse of the word 'sport' if fight fans are not given value for money. This seems to have occurred mostly with young heavyweights, no doubt due to the fact that the world heavyweight championship remains sport's richest prize. The dream of every fight manager and promoter is to discover a Dempsey, Louis, Marciano or Ali, but such fistic gods are few and far between. The careful handling of a young boxer is essential. The manager or promoter who causes a prospect to be prematurely bombed out is condemned as a heartless, money-grabbing pedlar of human flesh. A prospect is entitled to have a dozen or more contests against opponents in his own class plus a couple of tests against experienced 'has-beens'. But there are degrees as to how long a build-up should be allowed to go on, especially when the fighter is moving into big money for dismissing a long list of 'unknown warriors'. Most of us who have been around a long time can judge after a dozen fights or so against reasonable, if moderate, opponents whether a young fighter has the ability to become a champion. He should not expect to be protected for twenty or thirty contests. Boxing is a tough, rough, physical test and if the boxer has not got what it takes to get to the top he should be exposed. A phony build-up benefits only a handful of people with no interest other than making money.

Crooked fights with gangsters with one of the opponents

taking a dive belong to the distant past; they exist today only in the minds of fiction writers. Bud Schulberg's successful novel *The Harder They Fall* was based on the exploitation of the Italian giant Primo Carnera. Bud used his imagination to embellish the facts, but Carnera was in fact given a phony launch in America against a couple of dozen unknown opponents. Most of them were counted out inside one or two rounds. Gangsters guided him to the title and later abandoned him.

Fortunately those days are over. However, it is hardly creditable for a promoter to hire a suspect opponent in order to build up a young star or to rehabilitate a beaten champion with the full knowledge that the fighter chosen has been inactive for a long period and has been out of training and, therefore, not capable of giving the customers value for money.

The continual wrapping a champion in cotton wool is to be condemned. Cus D'Amato overprotected Floyd Patterson after he had become world heavyweight champion. In fairness to D'Amato, after Patterson won the Olympic middleweight gold medal at Helsinki in 1952, Cus guided him wisely as a professional to become heavyweight champion when Floyd knocked out Archie Moore, then in his forties. Luckily for Patterson, Marciano retired and Floyd, then only twenty-one, was the youngest-ever heavyweight champion. D'Amato proceeded to turn the heavyweight championship, so proudly held by Dempsey, Louis, Marciano and Ali, into a paper crown and the sport itself into burlesque, by hand-picking soft challengers, including Pete Radechmacher, an Olympic champion, making his professional debut. How could even the most naive boxing official take a world heavyweight title fight seriously when the challenger was participating in his first professional contest?

Another safe challenger was Brian London, who had been thrashed by Henry Cooper in a British title match. The British Boxing Board declined London permission to fight Floyd, but as the offer was worth nearly £20,000 to him he went to Indianapolis and was beaten in eleven rounds. The Board fined him £1000 but he was laughing. However, D'Amato tripped up a few weeks later. He thought the Swede Ingemar Johansson would be another 'victim'. But Ingemar knocked Floyd down seven times and knocked him out in the third round. Later Patterson twice knocked out the Swede. Cus D'Amato was, with some justification, trying to avoid Sonny Liston and chose another soft touch in Tom McNeely. Patterson stopped him in four rounds. By hand-picking too many of Patterson's challengers D'Amato cheapened the heavyweight championship.

The build-up of Gerry Cooney was carefully planned and profitable but did not bring the best out of Cooney. Gerry, standing 6 ft 5 in and weighing 16 st, was seen as the great white hope to end black dominance of the heavyweight title for the best part of fifty years since Louis knocked out Braddock in 1937. With the exception of Marciano, who remained undefeated, and Johansson, champion for one year, all the heavyweight kings since Braddock have been black.

Cooney was nursed along from 1977 to 1980 beating twenty-two almost anonymous opponents. He knocked out three big-named fighters, all of whom were over the hill, which enabled him to share a purse against Larry Holmes said to be worth $20 million. To his credit he fought bravely and by sheer strength made a fight of it. Yet in his twenty-sixth professional fight he still, in many ways, performed like a novice having learned little in his five years build-up of twenty-five contests totalling only eighty-six rounds. Cooney has a reach of 81 inches and a powerful left hook which he used mainly to the body. This was not enough to topple the experienced Holmes who almost knocked him out in the second round. By sheer guts, Gerry survived for nearly thirteen rounds before being battered to defeat.

Cooney had so many assets to become a champion – physique, reach, power and guts – but he also had two liabilities. He lacked a love for the fight game and was injury-prone. Fights were postponed because of a torn back muscle, a pulled shoulder muscle and various injuries to his hands. Having made a fortune, the Irish giant showed little desire at twenty-five to return to the ring. After twenty-seven months of idleness he stopped Phil Brown, a trial horse, in four rounds and three months afterwards halted George Chaplin, in two. He then lapsed into inactivity until in 1985, when there was talk of his coming back for another crack at Holmes's title. When Holmes made it clear he did not intend to give the Irishman a second chance to earn a fortune, Cooney lost interest and returned to obscurity.

But when Holmes lost the IBF title to Michael Spinks, Cooney once again emerged from the shadows to announce he was prepared to make a come-back if it led to a championship match with Spinks. In June 1968, after seventeen months absence, he bombed out a fair heavyweight, Eddie Gregg, in eighty-six seconds at San Francisco to cause a stir and justify a challenge to Spinks.

The build-up of Joe Bugner seemed as long-running as *The Mousetrap*. The Hungarian-born fighter was a perfect physical specimen with some of Cooney's assets. He stood 6 ft 3 in, weighed more than 16 stone and proved durable against good punchers. He also shared a similar weakness with Cooney. He loved the money boxing brought him but did not love fighting for the sake of it as Dempsey, Ali, Greb, Robinson, and many other great champions did.

He was knocked out in his first professional fight in 1967 by Phil Brown but was never again counted out in sixty-eight contests. Perhaps that first knockout in three rounds when only seventeen caused his extreme caution over the selection of future opponents. In the next two years he quickly defeated twenty-one of twenty-two opponents, including Phil Brown, but one of several moderate American opponents, Dick Hall, outpointed him over eight rounds. In 1970 he won all nine contests, mainly against has-beens. The following year, when he was just twenty-one, he caused a shock by taking the European, British and Commonwealth titles from Henry Cooper in a controversial decision. Yet six months later he performed like a novice. Jack Bodell, a clumsy southpaw, thrashed him over fifteen rounds to take the three titles. All Bugner's ten opponents in 1972 were carefully picked and he duly disposed of them inside the distance. This included the regaining of the European title against the German Jurgin Blin, who made a voluntary defence for £20,000, was knocked out in eight rounds and never boxed again.

Going to the other extreme, Bugner fought two losing but commendable bouts with Ali in Las Vegas and Joe Frazier in London. I rate his showing against Frazier as his best performance. But out came the cotton wool again and Joe was protected like a beginner, with eight soft opponents, two of whom, in fairness to Bugner's camp, were nominations of the European Boxing Union for Joe to defend the European title.

How could his camp justify starting a second build-up? He had become a mature heavyweight, having taken part in fifty-seven professional contests, won the European title twice and successfully defended it four times. He had also gone the distance with Ali and Frazier. The reason for the pussyfooting was that negotiations were going on for Bugner to meet Ali again, this time for the title, as the Greatest had become champion for a second time. To make this lucrative match it was essential for Bugner to remain undefeated. His easy knock-outs of a Mexican, Jose Luis Garcia, and an Argentinian, Alberto Lovell, each in two rounds, in the space of two months in 1974, were farces. Lovell, brought in as a late substitute, put up no resistance. Bugner tossed aside the European crown and went to Kuala Lumpur to challenge Ali for a £200,000 pay day. Because of the humidity in Malaysia the fight took place at breakfast time. Bugner seemed content to stay the distance for a second time with Ali. He stood like the Statue of Liberty allowing Ali to do most of the work without seriously getting hurt.

With Bugner apparently no longer interested in the British and European titles, there was a severe shortage of heavyweight talent in Britain and Europe. Jack Bodell, Danny McAlinden, Bunny Johnson and Richard Dunn held the title briefly. Dunn also took the vacant European crown, stopping a German hairpin, 6 ft 7 in Bernd August, in three rounds. This victory entitled Dunn to challenge Ali for the title in a one-sided five rounds at Munich. The Yorkshireman had not the slightest chance but grossed £100,000. Dunn was courageous and had a go, but it was still a mismatch with the Yorkshireman down five times. It was all over in 14 minutes 45 seconds, with Ali clowning and indicating to Dunn at the start of the fifth round that it would be the Yorkshireman's last round. Thus the rapid build-up of Dunn from an almost anonymous fighter into British and European champion and world challenger served no useful purpose for the sport other than to make a few people richer.

Bugner, seeing a chance to add to the £600,000 he had

grossed, showed interest in regaining the British and European titles and emphasized the falseness of Dunn's position as a world contender by flattening the Yorkshireman in 134 seconds at Wembley with the pair splitting £75,000. Having collected again, Bugner showed no further interest in either title.

Bugner remained almost inactive for three years and tried a comeback in 1982, only to be stopped in two rounds by Earnie Shavers. He then returned to London to take up Frank Warren's offer and won four televised fights against moderate opponents. When he quarrelled with Warren we were spared another Bugner build-up at thirty-three. He went back to America and was beaten by Marvis Frazier. He had lost to father and son, Joe and Marvis, in the same decade.

Billy Walker, golden boy of the sixties, was served a few cushy rivals but Billy was unable to win a professional title. Yet he was bigger at the box office than most British heavyweight champions. The danger of build-ups, apart from fooling the public, is that inevitably they lead to gross mismatches in order to make money. If Walker had not lost to Brian London, there would have been a good chance of matching him against Ali, though he would not have had the slightest chance of winning.

Frank Bruno, ABA heavyweight champion in 1980, served a most cautious apprenticeship. Terry Lawless, his manager, makes no apology. Bruno was turned down for a professional licence, having failed an eye test, but after a successful operation in South America he became a professional in 1982 and beat ten opponents of little standing in quick time. He beat another ten of a better grade in 1983 but Jumbo Cummings sounded a warning by almost knocking Frank out. The British fighter survived and won in seven rounds.

The question arose, could he take a big punch? More doubts came in his twenty-second fight when he was knocked out in the last round by James Bonecrusher Smith. Smith was certainly no pushover and Bruno had fought well until getting caught. After a rest he easily won the European crown by knocking out the Swede Anders Ecklund. His one-round crushing of the South African Gerrie Coetzee impressed the world. I was less impressed. I had seen Coetzee fight in South Africa. He was a good heavyweight but was now well over the hill having turned thirty, and Bruno had no trouble flattening him with a crushing right-hand punch. Coetzee promptly announced his retirement.

Bruno's sensational win lined him up with Tim Witherspoon and, I fear, the British media went hysterical, describing likeable Frank as another Sonny Liston with a killer punch and the fitness and strength of a super-being. They had forgotten his suspect chin and lack of stamina. He had never gone ten rounds, never mind the fifteen requested against Witherspoon.

I was extremely puzzled when bookmakers announced Bruno was favourite against Witherspoon, who had fought opponents in a different league and had never been knocked out or down by sharp punchers such as Larry Holmes, Greg Page, Bonecrusher Smith, Pinklin Thomas or Tony Tubbs. Some of his sparring partners in Philadelphia probably punched him as hard as Bruno. So what made so many think the inexperienced Frank could do what America's top heavyweights couldn't achieve?

Having said this, let me emphasize that Bruno was magnificent in defeat. He showed courage and was as fit as he could ever be. He also showed improvement, revealing a splendid left hook to the body, and handled himself with credit against a far more experienced champion. The whole of Britain was proud of him.

What does the future hold for Bruno? He can earn plenty and, I believe, could easily take the British title if he wants it and also regain the European crown, which he gave up to concentrate on the World title dream. He can still beat American opposition but I don't think he has the equipment to defeat the current three world heavyweight champions: Witherspoon, Michael Spinks or the veteran, Trevor Berbick. At twenty-four he has youth on his side, but America has already produced Mike Tyson, a twenty-year-old black New Yorker, undefeated in his first twenty-five contests. Of these, he has stopped twenty-three opponents and fifteen in the first round.

There will be more abortive build-ups in Britain and Europe as managers and promoters chase the prize worth millions of dollars, but right now the prospect of a home-born heavyweight achieving what Bob Fitzsimmons did one hundred years ago sadly seems as far away as ever.

Mismatches

While accepting that the build-up of a promising novice is essential so long as it is not abused, I blame managers who match a reasonably established fighter against a super-champion knowing their fighter has no chance of winning. They stand accused of grabbing a big pay day regardless of the outcome or of exercising bad judgement. It is the manager's duty to safeguard his fighter. However, it does not follow that a boxer who ends up being heavily beaten was mismatched. One punch can change the course of a fight and some of the heaviest punishment takes place when the contestants are well matched, as with Ali and Frazier in New York and Manila. Even the worst tragedy with one of the fighters dying has followed a well-matched pair. This was the case with Emile Griffith and Benny Paret, who met three times for the world welterweight title. Each scored a narrow points win but in the third fight Paret was knocked out and later died. Davey Moore was an outstanding featherweight champion but lost his world crown when knocked out by Sugar Ramos; he also died. Johnny Owen, from Wales, died weeks after being knocked out by the Mexican Lupe Pintor in Los Angeles. Johnny was undefeated British, Commonwealth and European champion. He had never previously taken the full count and had dropped only one controversial decision in twenty-seven bouts. The tragedy could not be blamed on a mismatch.

The sort of contests I criticized before the event were Freddie Mills *v.* Joe Baksi and Sugar Ray Leonard *v.* Dave Boy Green. Mills, a light-heavyweight, was asked to concede 28 lb to Baksi, a leading American heavyweight. He took a six-round beating. Green had no chance against undefeated super-champion Sugar Ray Leonard. Dave was a gutsy willing fighter with a suspect defence. He had made a tremendous earlier bid for the world title until getting knocked out by Carlos Palomino in 1979, but he was slipping. He lost the European title when flattened in three rounds by Jorgen Hansen, a thirty-six-year-old Dane, so what chance had he against the hard-hitting undefeated Leonard? He was knocked unconscious in four rounds when his head crashed on the canvas, but he was already out from Leonard's left hook before he fell. There was considerable anxiety at ringside as a doctor entered the ring when he did not recover immediately. Happily, Dave has suffered no ill effects and his share of a £50,000 purse has provided him with a comfortable retirement. But I remember that Leonard admitted it was the first time he felt fear after knocking out an opponent.

Quite a few of Louis's twenty-five defences were called 'Bum of the Month', while Ali had equally easy defences, but such super-champions would have become almost idle if they had waited until opponents with a chance of beating them were found. It must be said of Louis and Ali that neither ducked any challenger. They beat the best and worst heavyweights around. Both were so outstanding from the start that they did not need a phony build-up. The men to be blamed in some of their championship fiascos were the managers of the challengers. Unfortunately some managers allow the promoters to take over and talk them into fights which they must know in their hearts their fighter has no chance of winning.

Occasionally the experts can be quite wrong and what appears to be a bad match on paper turns into an upset like the Max Baer–Jim Braddock heavyweight championship or the first Sugar Ray Robinson–Randolph Turpin contest. There were similar surprises with Don Cockell against Jim Slade and Freddie Mills against Lloyd Marshall. Cockell was expected to take good care of Slade, a black American reckoned to be past his best, and then go on to meet Joey Maxim for the light-heavy crown. The Duke of Edinburgh was introduced to both fighters. Slade seemed inspired by such a royal greeting and knocked out Don, who had just started having weight problems. Mills was expected to dismiss Marshall on the way to a second title bout with Lesnevich, but the American bowled Freddie over in five rounds. If these two contests had gone the other way, I suppose with hindsight the knockers would have said the fights were crooked!

It would be unreasonable to blame promoters, matchmakers or managers just because fights turn out to be one-sided. Take the pairing of Don Curry, the undefeated WBA champion, with Milton McCrory, the WBC champion and also undefeated, for the undisputed welter crown in 1985. Bob Arum ballyhooed the match as 'the Toss-up'. Curry was favourite but was not expected to annihilate McCrory inside two rounds.

I could list scores of pairings of intriguing matches that became one-sided fights. Here is just a sample: Marciano–Walcott (second fight), Patterson–Liston (twice), Liston–Clay (twice), Frazier–Foreman and Foreman–Norton. Walcott and Marciano had had thirteen bloody rounds the first time they met. Rocky flattened Jersey Joe in one round in the return. Liston disposed of Patterson twice in under three minutes and then quit against Clay in six rounds and later was humiliated in the first round. Frazier was blitzed out of his title by Foreman in two rounds and Ken Norton, having beaten Ali, was savaged by Foreman in two rounds. Good matches, like marriages, are not always made in heaven!

Champions are allowed a voluntary defence before taking a challenger nominated by a controlling body and this can bring about a poor match, but sometimes the ruling association does not help. For instance, the European Boxing Union insisted that Barry McGuigan defend the European Championship against the moderate Frenchman Farrid Gallouze in 1985 despite protests from the BBBC. Gallouze put up no opposition and was beaten in two rounds. As a championship it was a farce.

In some cases the boxer himself persuades the manager into accepting a bad match, because he over-estimates his own ability or needs the cash. Few boxers come to terms with the fact that their best fighting days are over. That is why, from the days of Gentleman Jim Corbett down to Larry Holmes, only Tunney and Marciano retired as heavyweight champion and did not attempt a comeback. A first-class manager will not go along with a deteriorating fighter who insists on 'just one more fight'. It would be easy to shrug the shoulders and take the percentage but it is better to say, 'Enough is enough'. There lies the difference between the good and bad manager.

The good manager also needs to be an opportunist with a sense of timing. Terry Lawless has these gifts. The time for John H. Stracey to face Jose Napoles, an outstanding champion, in Mexico was perfect. Napoles had been a pro and was nearly thirty-six, yet most experts still backed him. He almost put Stracey out in the first round but John H. survived and Napoles had nothing left after six rounds. Stracey was world champion. Shrewd timing also brought the world lightweight title to Jim Watt when Roberto Duran gave up the crown. Sometimes the best of plans go wrong. You win some. You lose some.

Never Bet on Fights

In the early hours of 12 July 1961, Sam Silverman, a likable, corpulent, cigar-chewing promoter from Boston, left a night club off Piccadilly and was immediately beaten up. He was knocked down, punched and kicked. He had been in the West End club with his friend Elliot Price, one of Boston's big gamblers, a few hours after Terry Downes, a 7–4 underdog, had brought off a big upset by winning the world middleweight title from Paul Pender at Wembley. Six months earlier in Boston Downes had been stopped in seven rounds with a horrendous nose injury, but this time, to everyone's surprise, Pender had suddenly surrendered his world crown as, slumping on his stool, he declined to come out for the tenth round. It was a similar action to Sonny Liston's capitulation in the seventh round against Cassius Clay in their first fight at Miami three years later. In America world champions are expected to go down fighting, and if they give up on the stool they get hammered as quitters.

This second Pender–Downs affair had not been a thriller and there was little between them after eight rounds. The only visible damage was a slight cut under Pender's eye while Terry's left eye was puffy. The Boston champion had come out throwing punches in round 9, catching Downes with some good shots, and it looked as though he might begin to forge ahead as he took this round. Then, to everybody's astonishment, the champion's trainer, Al Lacey, called referee Ike Powell to the corner to say that Pender's eye was too bad for him to continue. Powell did not examine the eye but called Downes to the centre of the ring and raised his right hand. So far as the referee was concerned, the champion had retired. Later Lacey said that Pender had had injections for a severe cold a few days before the fight and was not fit to continue.

The gamblers who lost their cash screamed, 'Fix!' They always do. One disgruntled London gambler was Albert Dimes, a tough character seen regularly round the horse and dog tracks, boxing tournaments and gaming clubs, who had made headlines in a fight with the notorious Jack Spot in Soho. Dimes who had lost a large sum of money backing Pender, was wrongly convinced there had been a betting coup involving Silverman, Elliot Price and Pender, went to the night club and waited for Silverman and Price to take revenge.

When I heard about the attack later that morning, I called on Silverman, who was staying at the Carlton Towers Hotel. Sam's face was more bruised than Pender's and gently he lifted his trousers to show two badly bruised shins. He recognized Albert Dimes, a regular fight fan, as his attacker but did not wish to press charges. He was anxious to keep the news as quiet as possible. Elliot Price was not available to see me.

It had been an unsatisfactory ending to a world title fight. Terry Downes was, understandably, annoyed with Pender for quitting and more so with the bunch of cynics who always know a fight has been fixed the next day! Pender must come in for criticism for his action. He had not exactly gone down fighting.

In an exclusive interview after the fight Downes told me, 'I lost all respect for Pender the way he quit. A champion must defend his crown to the last ditch. He had demanded nearly £57,000, thirty feet of bandage on each hand. Furthermore, before he agreed to switching this second meeting from Boston to London his lawyer insisted that every penny of my £7000 purse should be deposited in an American bank to make sure that if I won the title I would have to meet him a third time in Boston.'

Terry was naturally angry with the rumours of a betting coup. 'What nonsense it all is,' he growled. 'The bookmakers made money. They were offering 8–1 against me winning between the sixth and tenth rounds. If somebody knew something, the bookies would have caught a cold. As for the guys who backed Pender and lost their dough, I couldn't care less.

Nobody asked them to bet on him or me. When I had half my nose mashed in Boston, some guys said I was outclassed. Now I've won the title they suggest it was bent. What a lot of rot. If Pender had licked me twice, he wouldn't have needed to meet me a third time. There was half a million bucks waiting for him to face Gene Fullmer, the National Boxing Association champion. The eye injury was nothing. When he had a go in the ninth round that was his last desperate stand and he could see he hadn't hurt me. Maybe the guy didn't feel good but he quit to avoid the indignity of a KO. He ruined a greater victory for me.'

My sympathies were with Downes. Fight gamblers are not sportsmen. Once their cash is on, they lose all sense of fair play, abuse the other guy and become prejudiced. They only see their man scoring points. Bad losers should never bet on fights.

The Downes–Pender three-fight series illustrates an unhealthy side of boxing in America in the days when no world champion would agree to risk losing his title without the challenger first signing a return-clause contract and often not getting his full purse till he had gone through with the second contest. Before Pender agreed to meet Downes the first time in Boston, Terry had to sign to give him a return fight within ninety days in Boston if he won the title. Downes would get only 15 per cent of the $65,000 television contract and 20 per cent of the receipts at Boston Arena, which worked out at around £7000. What was unfair was that Pender could demand more than Downes for the return fight even if Terry had won the first fight to become champion. Downes was not to be paid until he had fulfilled the second match. Furthermore, when Silverman agreed to allow the fight to take place at Wembley, he insisted on a cut of the promotion. It was a completely one-sided agreement, but unless Downes agreed there was no way he would get a shot at the world crown. Silverman and Pender agreed to allow the second fight to be switched to England as they realized it would draw more money than in Boston. Silverman was given a £7000 cut in on the Wembley promotion.

John Cronin, a prominent Boston lawyer who had helped draw up the contracts for some of Ali's most lucrative fights, looked after Pender's interests and he did a great job. It was he who had insisted on Downes's purse being held in escrow so that if successful, the British fighter had to return to Boston for a third fight. That is what Terry did in April 1962 and lost the decision and the title back to Pender. Both boxers were cut and bruised in a hard if not brilliant bout. Pender did a great deal of holding without the referee intervening.

Pender was smart to employ Cronin. The American system was so complicated that a good lawyer was more important to a fighter than a good manager and Cronin protected Pender from every conceivable angle. Sam Silverman, too, was a straight shooter of the old school. He had helped build up Marciano in Rocky's early days and refused to be intimidated by the hoodlums operating in the USA. Bullets had been fired through the window of his home and like Ray Arcel, the renowned trainer, he had been beaten up in Boston when he resisted hoodlum pressure. That is why he did not squeal when punched and kicked after the Downes–Pender clash in London. Sam believed in taking the rough with the smooth.

Pender never fought again. He was stripped of the title by every commission bar Massachusetts. He retired and took over a large bakery. John Cronin, though retired, travels the world to see fights. Sam Silverman and Albert Dimes have passed on and the last time I heard of Elliot Price, the big gambler had moved from Boston to Las Vegas where the casino bosses get richer as long as the high rollers keep rolling. Human nature does not change. Sixty years ago a blonde who ran a Chicago speakeasy during Prohibition greeted all her customers who queued to guzzle hooch with 'Hiya, suckers!' When will they ever learn?

# BOOK THREE

THE UGLY

Day of the Hoodlums

The disgrace of boxing in America for decades was the acceptance by some politicians that it was inevitable that racketeers and hoodlums would always move in and take over the sport. Though boxing is officially controlled by various state commissions, a few gangsters had far more power. Back in the twenties Al Capone, Lucky Luciano, Legs Diamond and others had a big influence on boxing. Many state commissioners turned a blind eye to the malaise, pretending or hoping that it did not really exist or that, if it did, it would eventually go away. The Chicago boys of the twenties and thirties did not need boxing financially but it gave them a kick to be seen at ringside and talking to the champions. Yet the worse period for infiltration of the underworld into US boxing took place in the forties, fifties and sixties when Franki Carbo and his loyal lieutenant Blinky Palermo from Philadelphia were the most influential undercover men in America.

Carbo had a long record of crime, including murder. He had a group of associates whom he put in charge of various fighters, including world champions, and influenced the International Boxing Club which had its headquarters at Madison Square Garden. Jim Norris, the IBC president and a business millionaire from Chicago, was sometimes seen in the company of the notorious Carbo, who struggled like all affluent gangsters to appear legitimate. Dressing in expensive grey suits, he became known in the underworld and boxing as 'the Man in Grey'. I met him only once at the Chateau Madrid, a New York night club, run in the fifties by Angel Lopez, one of the managers of

Kid Gavilan, the Cuban world welterweight champion. I was dining with Bill Daly, then riding high in the fight game in New York, and Bill introduced me to the Man in Grey. Had I not been aware of his sordid record, I would have accepted him as another fight manager. What struck me as almost childish was that whenever Carbo wanted to discuss anything private with Lopez or Daly they would disappear through a sliding panel in the dining-room wall, only returning when their business was settled.

There is little doubt that Carbo had more power than any other individual in New York boxing. He was able to control the movements of several world champions, even though the boxers themselves were not always consulted. He used any methods – bribery, bullying, threats, blackmail – and a few guys who tried to oppose his moving in were beaten up. Realizing that any promoter who has the heavyweight champion under contract, like Rickard with Dempsey and Jacobs with Louis, he had tried to muscle in on Louis and Marciano, without success. His opportunity came with the arrival of Sonny Liston in the early sixties. It was well known that both Carbo and Palermo were behind Liston. New York state refused Liston a licence to box because of his association with Carbo. His four title fights – against Floyd Patterson (twice) and Ali (twice) – went to Chicago, Las Vegas, Miami and Lewiston, Maine. Had Liston arrived on the scene ten or more years earlier than he did, Carbo and Palermo would have given American boxing a scar that would have stayed with the sport for ever. As it was, time was running out for Carbo.

In 1957 Jim Norris and Arthur M. Wirtz, president of Chicago Stadium, were found guilty of monopolistic practices by Judge Sylvester J. Ryan and were ordered to dispose of their stock in Madison Square Garden. He also ordered them to dissolve the IBC in New York and Chicago. Carbo remained free, if in the background; he hoped to become even more powerful when Liston became champion.

In December 1960 the hearings of a government investigation into professional boxing began in Washington before the Antitrust and Monopoly Committee of the Senate. The biggest names in boxing were called to give evidence and startling revelations about Carbo, Palermo and their associates were made in public for the first time. However, the credit for forcing Carbo and Palermo behind bars goes to the late Robert Kennedy, who, as Attorney General, brought extortion charges against the pair in California. They were found guilty and Carbo received a sentence of twenty-five years in prison. Palermo was sentenced to fifteen years and after a lengthy appeal was also sent to jail.

The publication of the findings of the Antitrust and Monopoly Commission hearing in Washington at last revealed how closely some established boxing promoters and managers had been working with the underworld. It was amazing how a wealthy businessman like Jim Norris allowed Carbo to dictate to him. A manager in California had fixed several fights, and the IBC had paid $45,000 in 'goodwill' payments to Mrs Carbo and $130,000 to the infamous Managers Guild. The guild was the brain child of Carbo to move in on the huge fees television was paying for fights but it became a dictatorial body threatening and bullying managers and fighters who declined to join.

Ike Williams, the former world lightweight champion, who once defended his title against the British champion, Ronnie James, in Cardiff, gave damning evidence against Palermo. Williams testified that when he parted from his old manager, Connie McCarthy, he was boycotted because he would not take on a manager belonging to the Guild. He could get no fights until he agreed to let Palermo manage him. Williams claimed that he had not received a penny of his last three purses under Palermo. Two of these purses were for $32,000 each and the third was for $12,000. He also alleged that four offers of bribes ranging from $30,000 to $100,000 had been made to him to lose contests. Hymie Wallman, a leading manager of the fifties, stated that Carbo practically controlled matchmaking for the IBC and although two world champions had managers, each fighter came indirectly under Carbo's control.

Senator Kefauver, who chaired the Senate committee, declared during the hearings that the recent conviction of Carbo, Palermo and others in the Californian court was due to the manner in which Robert Kennedy and his special prosecutor had presented the case. Carbo was escorted from prison to attend the hearings but pleaded the Fifth Amendment and refused to answer thirty questions; Palermo, who was on bail, declined to answer eleven of the questions put to him by the investigators.

Thus after years of riding roughshod over the law and the boxing commissions, the two leaders of an incredible boxing mafia were at last brought to justice. Carbo and Palermo were confident up to the final day of the trial in California that there would not be sufficient evidence to convict them. For years they had beaten the rap for outrageous boxing crimes. Carbo commented to a stooge who visited him in prison, 'They finally got me for spitting on the sidewalk!'

Such was the power of these two men that even after Carbo had begun his sentence and while Palermo was fighting his appeal their influence remained. Some hoodlums remained loyal to their boss and visited him in prison. There was no doubt he and Palermo still had influence over Liston but this was for a limited period. Kennedy had rid American boxing of its worst period of gangster control. Both mobsters are now dead.

Doc Kearns, the wily old hustler who had managed Dempsey, Mickey Walker, Joey Maxim and Archie Moore and dozens of other fighters, visited Carbo in jail and reported him to be a sick man. Doc, a survivor from the Roaring Twenties, told me he had also visited Capone in Alcatraz years earlier and found Public Enemy Number One an ailing sad old man. Kearns never professed to being an angel, as he revealed in his autobiography *Larceny is My Business*, but was a likable character who managed to keep on the right side of the law. He died an old man.

Bill Daly, a friend of Kearns and an associate of Carbo and Palermo, also lived to past eighty. Bill, like Kearns, always kept one step ahead of the law and, though interviewed by the FBI, was never indicted. Like Kearns, he was a tough, affable character who, though he moved in the company of hoodlums, was never classed as one. I had met him before the war when he arrived in England apparently having had to leave America for 'personal' reasons. He lived in London and managed fighters here. His best prospect was Maurice Strickland, the heavyweight champion of New Zealand. The only time Bill revealed his tough side was when a decision was given against Strickland in favour of the German Walter Neusel at Wembley Arena in 1937. It was a bad verdict and the crowd booed for a long time. The incensed Daly rushed to Neusel's dressing room and attacked Neusel's manager, Paul Damski. He wrongly believed the decision had been fixed. He claimed that Neusel hid under the table, not unreasonably as the angry Daly had a pair of scissors in his hand. The BBBC rightly suspended him from British boxing and he returned to the States. Arthur Elvin, the Wembley boss, never promoted another boxing tournament.

I did not see Daly again till I went to New York for one of the Louis championships. He was managing Lee Savold and wanted to bring him to England to fight Bruce Woodcock more than a year after Bruce had been beaten by Joe Baksi. Savold met Woodcock twice. He was disqualified in 1948 for a controversial low punch and in 1950 stopped Bruce in four rounds in Britain's biggest post-war promotion at White City. Joe Louis had retired and while America matched Ezzard Charles and Jersey Joe Walcott for the vacant world title, Britain gave the Savold–Woodcock bout that label. Daly, who had been pardoned for his 1937 conduct at Wembley, behaved impeccably, as did Savold, while in Britain.

Like Doc Kearns, Bill Daly was no angel. The son of an Irish immigrant who died at an early age from alcoholism, Bill survived on the streets of Philadelphia by stealing food and lumps of coal. He drifted into the gyms and clubs of Philadelphia where a rough bunch were grafting to survive.

Despite some of the company he kept, Bill Daly had many good qualities. He talked straight, was loyal to his friends, even the bad guys! In fact, I found him more trustworthy, giving straight answers to questions, than many boxing folk who claimed to be legitimate operators. But boxing for too long was more of a racket than a sport in the United States and unless firm control is kept on professional boxing, which is now worth millions of dollars with the advent of television coverage, there will be new racketeers ready to move in.

Exploitation

In every walk of life some folk are exploited by other folk, who not only survive but often thrive through the hard work of someone else. It is all about ruthlessness, greed and man's inhumanity to man. Boxing provides the opportunity for the unscrupulous to exploit young men, with perhaps more brawn than brain, who start out believing they can punch their way to a fortune. Only talented fighters reach the top. Others inevitably end up disillusioned. There is less exploitation in British boxing today than forty or fifty years ago. Managers are now vetted more closely and the British record is still far ahead of America's where some state commissions are barely competent to deal with the complex characters involved in the fight game.

One could look back over the years and name scores of boxers in the United States, badly handled by unprincipled managers, who ended their careers prematurely dumped on the scrap heap through being overmatched or tossed into the arena too often. Even world champions like Primo Carnera, Joe Louis, Henry Armstrong, Beau Jack and Ezzard Charles were victims. Carnera was taken over by gangsters in the thirties. After winning and losing the heavyweight title, he finished his boxing career alone in a Brooklyn hospital, partially paralysed and broke. The Italian giant made a financial recovery in a phony wrestling world but, a sick man, returned in 1967 to die where he was born at Sequals in Italy sixty years earlier. The rise and fall of Carnera was a disgrace to American boxing.

Joe Louis was such a great fighter he could never be exploited inside the ropes, but poor old Joe was let down by people he

Benny 'Kid' Paret, of Cuba, is battered by Emile Griffith in their third clash for the world welterweight crown in 1962. Paret was knocked out in the twelfth round and carried from the ring on a stretcher in a coma. He died in a New York hospital

Terry Downes, despite a bruised and cut left eye, fights back against world middleweight champion Paul Pender at Wembley in 1961. The shock came when Pender quit at the end of the ninth round sitting on his stool. Trainer Al Lacey declared his eye was too bad to continue

'This ain't no jive; Cooper will fall in five!' Cassius Clay, the twenty-one-year-old new sensation and rhyming prophet, forecasts Cooper's fate and Henry is amused at the weigh-in for their first contest in 1963 at Wembley

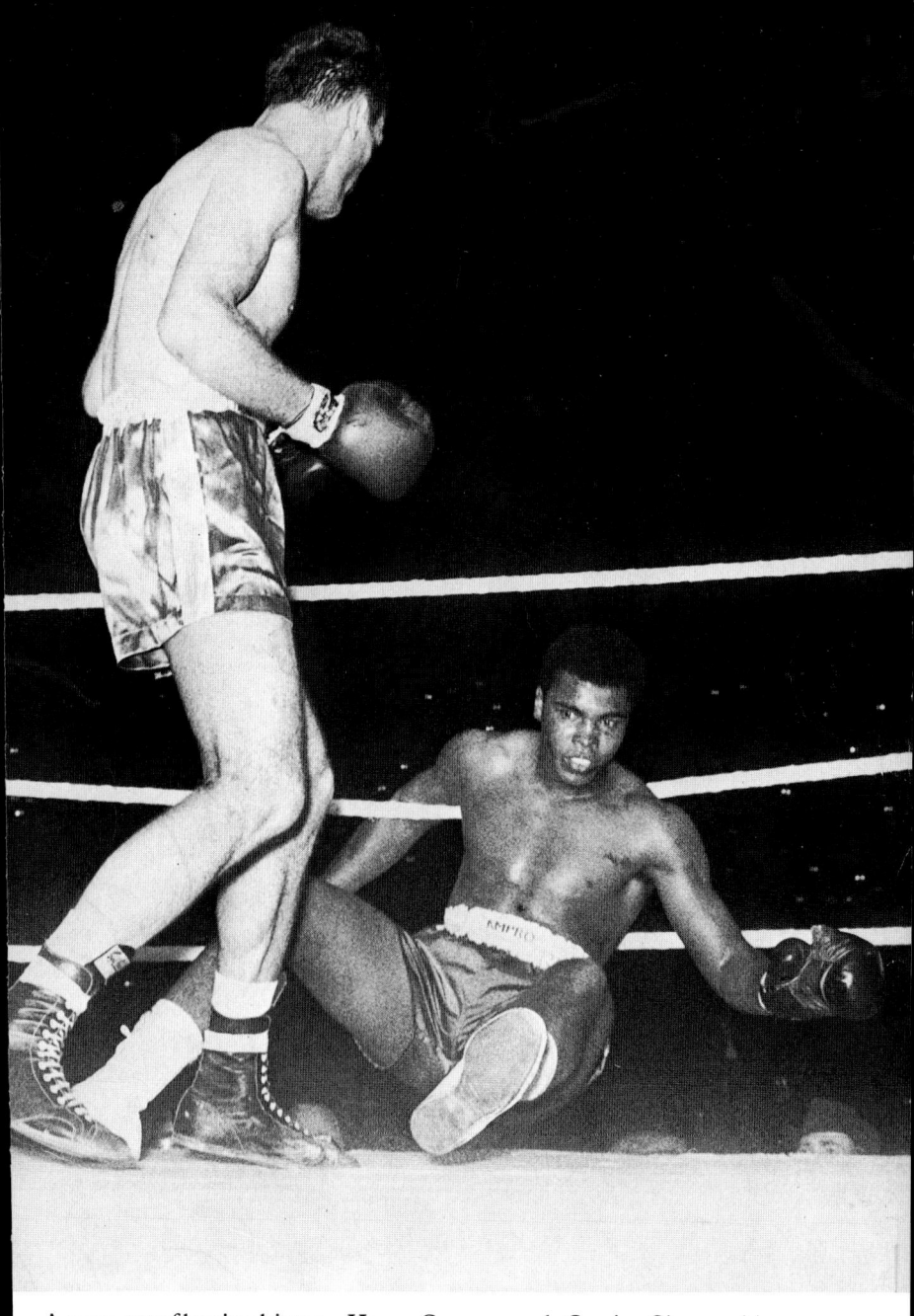

A moment of boxing history. Henry Cooper sends Cassius Clay crashing at the end of the fourth round at Wembley Stadium in 1963. The bell saved Clay and a split glove helped him with an extra half-minute to recover. But Henry's badly cut left eye caused referee Tommy Little to stop the fight in round 5

Above left: Britain's best lightweight, Ken Buchanan wins the British title knocking out Maurice Cullen in eleven rounds in 1968. The Scot won the world championship in Puerto Rico and successfully defended it several times in the United States

Above right: Johnny Owen, who won the British bantam title stopping Paddy Maguire beneath the chandeliers of the Cafe Royal in London

Below: Winstone – world champion at last. After three tremendous but abortive challenges against Mexican Vicente Saldivar, Howard Winstone wins the vacant world featherweight title stopping Mitsunori Seki (Japan) in nine rounds at the Albert Hall, London, in 1968

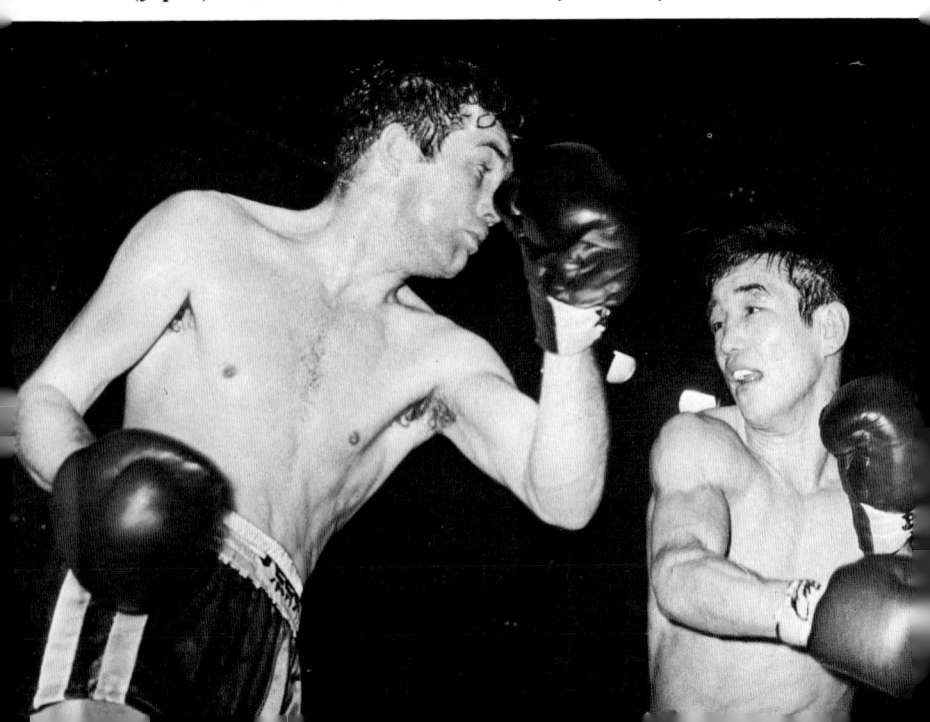

Above left: Breakfast at Caesar's: the inimitable Joe Louis, condemned to a wheelchair following a stroke and open heart surgery, touches the paper crown of Young Pretender Ken Norton for a press call at Las Vegas. Norton had been awarded the title. Louis died three years later

Above right: Jumping for joy: Roberto Duran leaps into the air with the announcement he has beaten Sugar Ray Leonard for the welterweight crown at Montreal in 1980

Below: Dave 'Boy' Green, Britain's brave welterweight champion, was knocked unconscious by Carlos Palomino after a tremendous challenge for the world title in 1977. After losing the European crown on a three rounds KO by Jorgen Hansen two years later, Green was badly mismatched against Sugar Ray Leonard for the world title again in 1980. Dave was knocked unconscious in four rounds but happily, after a doctor climbed into the ring, recovered and has shown no ill effect. But this fight should never have taken place

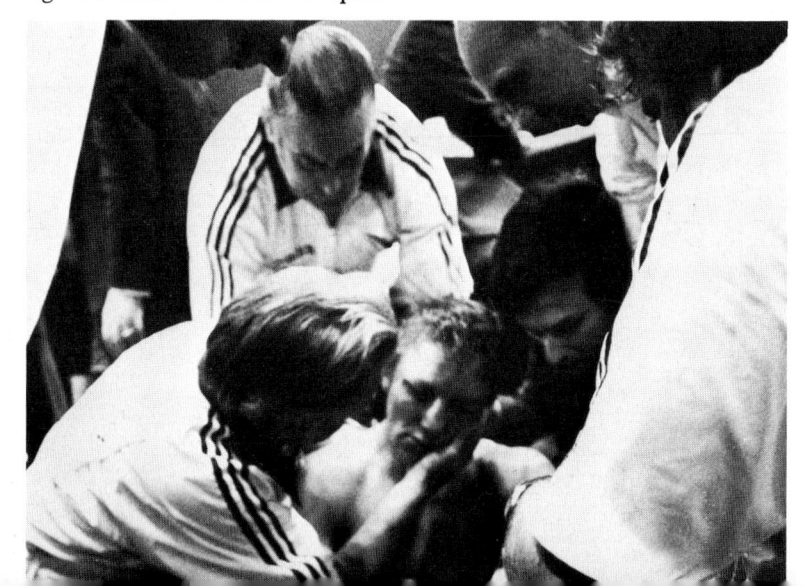

In 1962 George Walker, a retired boxer struggling with a mortgage on a garage in the East End, brought his kid brother Billy to the author's office with the exclusive news that Billy was to turn professional. In 1981 the Eastenders return for another interview as tycoons — George the millionaire chairman of Brent Walker, Billy as a tax exile in Jersey. The business was built up by George from the £250,000 Billy grossed from boxing without winning a title

Alan Minter is cut up by Marvin Hagler and loses his title to the American when the fight at Wembley is stopped by the referee in the third round

The manager and handlers of Marvin Hagler rush to protect him after he has won the world middleweight title from Alan Minter, and beer bottles are tossed at him from a few hooligan fans in the Wembley crowd. A Boxing Board inquiry followed. The author is at the ringside phoning a story of the violence

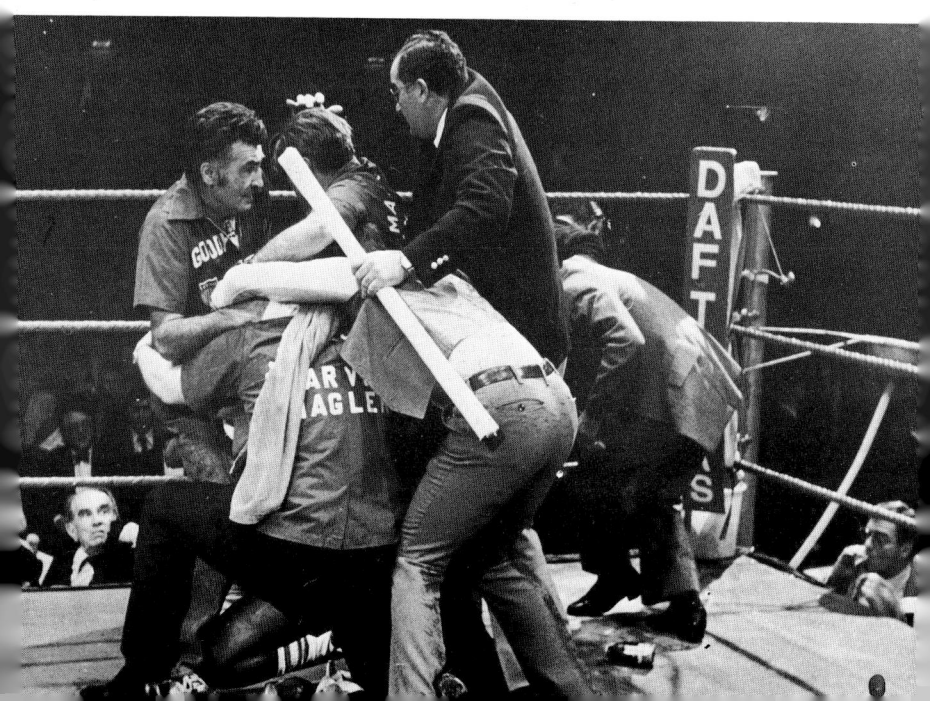

Barry McGuigan began sprightly when defending the WBA featherweight championship against America's Steve Cruz in the dazzling sunshine at Las Vegas in 1986. But the desert heat and the jabs of Cruz got to him in the closing rounds when he was floored several times to lose the decision and the title. A serious mistake was made agreeing to fight at the hottest time of the day

Brave Frank Bruno steps back to avoid a right swing from Tim Witherspoon, the WBA champion, at Wembley Stadium. Bruno put up a tremendous challenge but it turned out to be the impossible dream when he was stopped by the tough American champion in the eleventh round

thought were friends. He had no head for cash. His fists grossed $4.5 million. Yet in retirement after an enforced comeback he owed nearly $2 million in unpaid tax which he believed had been settled from purses. He joined the US Army in 1942 and was discharged nearly four years later. He defended his title twice during that period and each time donated his purse to the Navy and Army Relief Funds. Yet though he never earned again until he fought Billy Conn in 1946, his tax debts were going up by nearly $100 a day in 1956! He made a comeback and cheapened himself, taking part in wrestling bouts and television quiz shows, but all the time his debts were increasing. Louis finished his days a pathetic man, living with financial help from gamblers in Las Vegas. Worse was to come when his health collapsed. Quite a few individuals made a fortune out of Louis when he was the most feared fighter in the world. It is scandalous that he was betrayed by people he trusted.

Few champions have ended in more tragic circumstances than Ezzard Charles. Charles succeeded Louis and was a most under-rated boxer. Though he earned more than $2 million he ended his career broke. He had 122 contests in nineteen years and carried on fighting too long after he was through as a topliner. He finally gave up at thirty-eight but developed multiple sclerosis seven years later and spent the last nine years of his life paralysed in a wheelchair. Charles did not deserve so much suffering. He was a decent man. He never smoked or drank alcohol and lived quietly. He fought in the shadow of his idol, Louis, and once said, 'I hope I never see Joe beaten. He was too great.' Ironically, it was Charles who reluctantly humiliated the old Brown Bomber. He was an excellent boxer, perhaps too gentle by nature to be a super-champion.

I reckoned his best performance was when he lost over fifteen rounds against Marciano in 1954. It was a murderous fight. He nearly split Rocky's nose in half. But the punishment he took finished him as a top fighter. He went in again with Marciano three months later and was knocked out in eight rounds. From then on it was nearly all downhill. He lost fourteen of twenty-four bouts against moderate opposition and should never have been allowed to continue fighting. It would have been a kindness to suspend him. What happened to all those people who claimed to be his friends when he was heavyweight champion? His years of suffering ended when he died in Chicago. He was fifty-four.

Sugar Ray Seales, a twenty-year-old middleweight from Tacoma in Washington State, was the only American boxer to win a gold medal in the 1972 Olympics in Munich. He seemed set for a bright future. When he retired in 1983 after sixty-five professional contests he was broke and almost blind. A testimonial was held for him at the 25,000-seater Tacoma Dome. Ali, Hagler, Sammy Davis Junior all turned up but only 5000 tickets were sold and the show lost $20,000. The medical bills for treatment including operations for detached retinas to both eyes had mounted to around $90,000. Seales had no complaint against his manager, who helped organize the ill-fated testimonial. The boxer never revealed that he could hardly see out of his left eye until shortly before being forced to quit.

Seales must take a great deal of responsibility for his sad predicament. He was winning more fights than he was losing against moderate opposition and was concealing from doctors in various states that he had problems with his eyes but it seems that some of the medical examinations were not too thorough. He paid dearly for continually putting himself at risk. The only good news is that it was reported in 1985 that he had undergone further surgery, and although his left eye remains almost blind, his right eye has improved considerably.

The unfortunate Puerto Rican middleweight Willie Classen was another boxer who, because of need for cash, concealed health problems. He and his manager gave wrong information to commissions, saying he had been stopped by a cut eye when in fact he had been knocked out. He slipped through medical checks, more than once but paid for it when he died after getting knocked out in New York in 1979.

Back in the thirties and forties black fighters in the United States were unquestionably exploited by their white bosses. Henry Armstrong and Beau Jack should have ended up wealthy senior citizens. But black kids, escaping poverty from the Deep South, did not argue with promoters or managers and those who earned big money could not handle it and had nobody to advise them. Beau Jack (real name Sidney Walker) started as a shoeshine boy in Augusta, Georgia. He won the lightweight championship in the forties. The last time I heard of him he was back shining shoes at a Miami hotel on his sixty-fifth birthday.

Between the two wars fighters had to be really tough both in Britain and America. There were few safety measures and it is testimony to the toughness of that generation of fighters that they took part in hundreds of fights and survived to a good age. Jack Britton, who met Britain's Ted Kid Lewis twenty times, had more than three hundred contests. So did Johnny Dundee, while Harry Greb, Maxie Rosenbloom, Battling Levinsky, Freddie Miller, Fritzie Zivic and Sugar Ray Robinson all topped two hundred bouts. British fighters also had marathon careers. For instance, Len Wickwar, a splendid lightweight from Leicester, took part in 462 recorded contests despite being inactive for four war years. In 1934 he figured in fifty-eight contests, more than Henry Cooper had in his career of nearly eighteen years. Bill Bird, a likable Chelsea taxi driver, and George Marsden had well over three hundred bouts. Kid Lewis was not far short of this figure and Jack Kid Berg had nearly two hundred fights. While Len Harvey and Tommy Farr had more than a hundred recorded contests, each claimed they had fought in more than three hundred bouts, having started boxing for shillings at the age of twelve.

This could not happen in Britain today. A young boxer would not be allowed to fight two or three times a week, certainly not as a schoolboy. A boxer has to be eighteen before obtaining a full professional's licence and cannot become an apprentice pro until seventeen when he must box at the discretion of the British Boxing Board. While over eighteen but under nineteen, he is not permitted to box more than thirty minutes in any contest. The maximum number of rounds for a championship has been reduced from fifteen to twelve and anyone knocked out must be medically checked before boxing again. He is liable to suspension after losing four consecutive bouts. There is now a meticulous use of brain scans and thorough eye tests. In 1985 David Pearce, the British heavyweight champion, had his licence withdrawn following an abnormality revealed by a brain scan. Pearce fought a long legal battle to get his licence back. This was understandable as boxing was his only livelihood but surely for his own safety he should not be allowed to risk permanent injury or even death?

Fighters sometimes have to be protected from themselves.

All is not yet perfect. Mistakes have been made and will be made again, but it would not be possible today to exploit a brilliant teenager such as the remarkable Nipper Pat Daly who began as a pro at eleven and was finished at seventeen, having fought a hundred contests including five British champions. He was only sixteen when he was knocked out by the mature British featherweight champion Johnny Cuthbert in nine rounds in 1929. This was a disgraceful mismatch.

Freddie Mills was sometimes overmatched. It was partly his own fault because, though he fought as a light-heavyweight, the big cash was among the heavyweights. But there is no doubt that Mills became disenchanted with his manager Ted Broadribb, who was also his father-in-law. Freddie put his own cynical words to the tune of 'There's No Bizness Like Show Bizness'. His version went like this:

> There's no bizness like the fight bizness,
> They smile when they're hit low;
> All the managers are such schemers,
> Twenty-five per cent is all they know.
> Managers go on for blinkin' ever
> But where, oh where, do fighters go?

Fight managers are in boxing to make as much cash as quickly as possible, but, in fairness, some fighters are their own worst enemies. They, too, want to get rich quickly and attempt to hide a medical problem, as Sugar Ray Seales and William Classen did. This is where the good manager will take control and refuse to tolerate a boxer who tries to conceal his injuries. He will also hold back a youngster until he is ready to take on higher-grade opponents. Such a manager deserves 25 per cent of the fighter's purse, though it seemed a tough deal when Marciano allowed his mentor Al Weill to take 50 per cent of his gross earnings. Fighters come and go but managers go on and on. Doc Kearns, Jack Hurley, Bill Daly and Jim Wicks were still operating young fighters successfully at nearly eighty.

Henry Cooper has nothing but praise for the late Jim Wicks. Says Henry, 'He may have been old but his brain kept young till he died. Nobody could put one over Jim and he looked after me and taught me so much. As managers go, he was the greatest.'

Not all ex-boxers speak so highly of former managers. There

is no doubt that some have deserted old champions who have fallen on bad times. I could name many ex-fighters who were badly exploited by greedy managers and later abandoned – particularly in America. The breed of manager who screamed, '*We* ain't hurt' or '*We* wuz robbed' never used the plural when things went wrong. It was never a case of '*We* ended broke and blind.' Fortunately, there are not too many of that kind around today.

King Con

I have met so many con men in my time that now I can smell them before they come within talking distance. Boxing, like any big-money sport inevitably attracts them. At least con men do not survive for long as promoters, managers or fighters. The biggest con in boxing was the mysterious Mr Smith who promised to put the two most powerful boxing promoters in America, Don King and Bob Arum, out of business. Harold J. Smith, a 6 ft 2 in black man, heavily bearded beneath either a J. R. Ewing hat or a baseball cap and wearing cowboy boots, was an odd mixture of extrovert and introvert. He arrived on the fight scene as 'Mr Big' at the end of the seventies but remained elusive and eccentric. He completely shook American boxing by offering the boxers and their managers fantastic, in fact ridiculous, purses, which meant he would, and did, lose millions of dollars on promotions. He seemed to have a bottomless bank account. In a strange way, he had. The fight boys rubbed their hands and said that the guy was either a philanthropist or crazy but they did not care so long as he paid them fees which had Arum and King gasping.

He moved from Alabama to California, changed his name from Ross Fields to Harold J. Smith and joined the black freedom marches. Though not a Muslim, he became a personal supporter of Ali when the heavyweight champion was in trouble with the US Government for declining to join the army at the time of Vietnam. He was wise to cultivate Ali in the sixties and seventies when Ali's name was magic. Ali was more famous worldwide than Frank Sinatra, Elvis Presley or the President of the United States.

Ali seemed impressed by the young entrepreneur who apparently had run a few unsuccessful rock concerts in California. Harold J. Smith succeeded in persuading Ali, approaching the end of his fabulous career, to lend his name to a boxing promotion called MAPS (Muhammad Ali Professional Sports) with lavish headquarters at Santa Monica. Ali was not required to invest cash into the new organization or even become a director. He was promised $1 million for the use of his name. Ali was naive not to inquire where all the money was coming from. Harold J. Smith had been broke in the early sixties and when he first became a promoter he did not have the price of an air ticket from Los Angeles to New York. But his new lifestyle convinced the fight boys that he was loaded with gold and the managers and boxers welcomed being told that he and his wife and wealthy associates had put aside $12 million as working capital for MAPS.

If Harold J. Smith was not a millionaire, he certainly lived like one. He had a luxurious home at Pacific Palisades where Ronald Reagan once lived, owned a race horse and a power boat, and hired executive jets to fly him round America. He owned two convertible limousines while his wife Lee drove a Mercedes. He also escorted a bevy of pretty girls, known as 'Ali's Angels', on his jets just to parade the numbers between the rounds at his various tournaments. He always carried vast sums in $100 notes in an executive briefcase and wherever he went was accompanied by bodyguards. He had two partners but little was known about them.

Mr Smith set about challenging Arum and King by showering green dollars like tickertape from skyscrapers in a Manhattan parade. He also promised to end the conflict of the WBC and the WBA with two world champions in nearly every division. Smith called for one undisputed champion at each weight. In his initial promotion at Santa Monica boxing's new promoter paid the boxers double the gate receipts and lost $6000. Nine promotions later he lost $1 million. Yet Mr Smith did not appear concerned. It seemed there were still millions of dollars to come.

Mr Smith was shy of meeting newspapermen and I was anxious to interview him when I heard he was in Las Vegas for the Ali–Holmes fight. He had just announced an $8 million promotion at Madison Square Garden with three world championships on the one bill. Even the toughest US fight managers were predicting that if he succeeded with this promotioon without going bankrupt he might seriously have Arum and King on the run.

Bill Daly had flown in from Puerto Rico to where he had moved when things became awkward for him in New York State. Bill then in his eighties still enjoyed hustling, working with Don King. 'Have you ever met Mr Smith?' asked Daly, and when I told him I had been trying to get an interview he said, 'I've got a meeting with him at 10 a.m. tomorrow. The guy's dishing out millions. Why don't you come along?'

We duly arrived at the rendezvous at 10 o'clock. It was a luxury apartment way down the Strip. We were met by Smith's minders, hefty guys, who did not frisk us but followed us about. Mr Smith kept us waiting for twenty minutes but when he appeared, wearing a huge Texan cowboy hat and high boots, he was impressive, charming and articulate. On being introduced to me, a newspaperman from England, he said he liked London very much and would be going there perhaps to discuss a match with John L. Gardner, British and European champion. When I sought more information about the high purses he was paying, he managed to talk of anything but boxing! He was equally evasive with Daly, obviously aware that he had connections with King. Bill, who was managing a few fighters in Puerto Rico, wanted to get on the gravy train with some of those high purses but the fighters Daly managed did not interest Harold J. Smith. Bill, who had met them all, the entrepreneurs, the gangsters and the con men, accepted Mr Smith as a rich young man who enjoyed squandering his millions. Boxing's first philanthropist!

Within a few months of meeting Mr Smith, the scandal broke. Ali, at last suspicious as to where the money was coming from, demanded his name be no longer associated with MAPS. Suddenly the Madison Square Garden $8 million tournament, which Smith had ironically labelled 'This Is It', was cancelled. The promoter disappeared with the FBI looking for him. Wells Fargo National Bank of California reported $21 million had been embezzled from its Beverly Hills and Santa Monica branches. The bank was suing Smith and two MAPS directors. One worked at the Beverly Hills branch. Bob Arum summed up the crazy situation with a laugh: 'I once asked Smith about his endless supply of cash and all he would say was that it came from a legitimate source. What could be more legitimate than a bank?'

All three directors of MAPS later pleaded guilty to the embezzlement. The former manager of the Beverly Hills branch, who had gone missing, gave himself up and volunteered evidence against his two colleagues. Ali was completely innocent of MAPS' fraudulent transactions and the Madison Square Garden management was not involved. The arena had been hired for the night by Smith for his extravaganza and nearly $750,000 in advance sales had to be returned.

The bubble had burst. Don King and Bob Arum began to relax. Arum declared, 'A fighter worth $250,000 will be paid $250,000. If he wants $1 million, he had better go and find another Harold J. Smith.'

Though boxing had been given yet another black eye through the $21 million scandal, the sport itself was not implicated in the fraud. When Harold J. Smith planned to rob Wells Fargo Bank by tampering with computers, he might well have spent the money on racing, rock concerts or athletics. Boxing, unfortunately, attracts con men, but I think it will be a long time before it sees another Harold J. Smith.

Violence Outside the Ring

Marvin Hagler had just become the new middleweight champion of the world. He had badly lacerated the face of Britain's Alan Minter. Blood poured from cuts around Minter's eyes. As Panamanian referee Carlos Berrocol led the wounded Minter to his corner Doug Bidwell and Alan did not protest against the end of hostilities after three rounds of facial mutilation. Then suddenly all hell broke lose at Wembley.

As the shaven-headed Hagler went down on his knees in thanksgiving, just as Bjorn Borg used to do after another Wimbledon triumph, a few nasty troublemakers unleashed their anger on the new black world champion. Beer bottles, both plastic and glass, were showered at him as he sat crouched on the canvas. His managers body and Pat Petronelli and friend and lawyer Steve Wainwright gathered in a rugby scrum to protect him. And, believe me, I did not feel too happy as I phoned the story from ringside amid the disgraceful scenes with missiles crashing into the ring. The police acted promptly, entering the ring to escort the American champion to his dressing room. Hagler and his party would not have made it unscarred without them. The brief contest had been violent, punishing and tense, but fair. It was the unnecessary and unfortunate bitterness in the build-up before the fight *outside* the ring that had helped to whip up hate among the riff-raff, a very small minority, but it was the worst display by a boxing crowd in many, many years.

Though the media described it as yet another black eye for the most controversial of sports, boxing itself could hardly be blamed. For more than a quarter of a century we have witnessed the breakdown of law and order in our society; football hooliganism has become a part of our way of life as it gradually destroys Britain's once great national game. In fact, it seems remarkable that a sport as jingoistic as boxing should have steered almost completely clear of crowd and racial violence, especially as so many contests in Britain are now black *v.* white, but both races have behaved themselves and boxing crowds have a remarkably good record when it comes to law and order. There has been the odd exception. We had a period in the forties when the betting boys became a nuisance, roaming round the ringside and abusing the fighter they had not backed, but there was no violence. The Hagler–Minter obscenity was unique. Unfortunately it sowed the seeds for a few racist idiots to cause trouble at one or two subsequent tournaments.

Looking back on the Hagler–Minter fight, there seems little doubt that the troublemakers in the crowd wanted to believe that all the blood flowing from Minter's face was caused by butts from the American, but this was not the case. Minter, like Henry Cooper and Bruce Woodcock, could be easily cut around the eyes mainly because of his bone structure. Although plastic surgery can help, some fighters are always prone to being cut badly.

The real trouble over this fight was begun, encouraged and inflamed by one or two newspaper stories long before the fight took place. There was no attempt to play down the hostility between the two boxers because it provided stories and sold tickets. The antagonism apparently arose after an incident in Las Vegas when Hagler was challenging Vito Antuofermo for the world title. Minter, with a future interest, went along as a spectator and he and Hagler did not get on. Hagler declined to shake Alan's hand, which did not endear him to the British champion. Kevin Finnegan, who had lost three controversial decisions against Minter and had been stopped twice with cuts by Hagler, said the American had also refused to shake his hand. This, of course, was meat and drink to those wanting to stir up racist problems and rumours went around that Hagler had declared, 'I don't touch white flesh.' The American denied this and insisted he had shaken Finnegan's hand after he had beaten him and would shake any fighter's hand, white or black, he might face in the ring.

Hagler, unlucky to get a draw against Antuofermo, was annoyed that Minter was given the next shot at the title which Alan won on a split decision in Las Vegas. By the time the match was made between Minter and the American at Wembley hate stories were appearing in papers and magazines. Minter was quoted, 'I don't intend allowing a black man to take away my title.' He explained that he had been misunderstood in the quote and certainly was not in any way racist. He regretted the interpretation. But the damage had been done and with exaggerated stories flying around, some National Front extremists, who cause trouble at soccer games, decided to get in on the act. An American magazine reported inaccurately that Minter was a supporter of their movement. Alan denied these unjustified rumours, but the whole affair had been stoked up into a racist battle and was like a cauldron ready to boil over by fight time.

In view of all the trouble stirred up before the fight, Alan was perhaps unwise to allow himself to be persuaded to wear Union Jack trunks. Promoters Mike Barrett and Mickey Duff, understandably delighted with a sellout, went beyond the usual fanfare of trumpets and the dimmed lights for the entry of the gladiators. They hired a small band of Royal Marines with trumpets and in full military dress to blast the antagonists into the ring. A large Union Jack and a St George of England flag carried by a bearer draped in red, white and blue led Minter to the scene of battle. The black challenger, escorted by a bearer carrying the Stars and Stripes, made his way to ringside with both arms resting on the shoulders of Goody Petronelli. Apart from the few thugs who had filled their sumps with beer and spirits, the rest of us were wound up to a Saturday night fever and I felt my fingers tingling as I gripped my telephone. A section of the crowd were bellowing 'Minter! Minter! Minter!' Then came the two national anthems. Minter stood to attention and sang. Both men adopted the intimidating glare of hate introduced by Sonny Liston and exaggerated by Ali. It was the most tense pre-fight scene I can recall.

It was ringside ballyhoo at its best, in the style that Jack Solomons and the Greyhound Racing Association had staged at the great fights at Harringay and White City in the late forties and fifties. Only afterwards did everybody become wise and blame the build-up and the presentation for the violence.

Minter was keyed up. On occasions in the past he had lost his cool a little and impetuously had gone into a brawling battle rather than use his considerable boxing skill. When winning the world title he had shown patience and control, and he intended using similar tactics against Hagler. But the aggression got to him and he went out to win a quick war. Hagler was equally tense, realizing that only a handful of the crowd was on his side. So the two southpaws began tossing rights and crossing with their lefts and the crowd loved it, roaring for three minutes. Minter won the first round but his tactics were wrong. Hagler was icy cool, sticking his ripping right jab continually into the British fighter's face, which was already raw pink, and as he returned to his corner, a trickle of blood dripped from Minter's left eye. Alan went on the attack again in the second round but the Hagler fists were cutting him up and blood was pouring from around his left eye and from his nose. As the third round began it was clear that Minter would not be able to continue for long. Blood was gushing out with Hagler jabbing coolly but cruelly. The riff-raff section were getting angry and booing, blaming the Minter cuts on clashes from Hagler's head. A right uppercut from Marvin sent Minter's head back and blood sprayed across the ring. The referee stepped between them and led the British boy to his corner, minus his world crown. Then the hate boys vented their spleen and showered the ring with the nearest missiles – mostly beer containers.

Bob Arum, who was there to do a deal with the winner for the next big fight, angrily called out to me, 'This is disgraceful. You'll never get another American fighter to appear here.' Arum was justified. Most British boxing writers grabbed for their clichés and described it as Wembley's 'night of shame', as indeed it was. But when the adrenalin ceased to flow tempers cooled. The British Boxing Board rightly showed alarm and called a special meeting. Leading boxing writers were invited to comment. The Board showed more responsibility than either the Football Association or the Football League, which dillydallied for too many years after soccer violence began in the sixties.

Unpleasant displays followed at the National Exhibition Centre in Birmingham when Colin Jones was beaten in four rounds by Don Curry, the black WBA welterweight champion, early in 1985, and later when Azumah Nelson of Ghana, the WBC featherweight champion, knocked out Pat Cowdell in the first round. A few louts had been drinking and showed their displeasure at Jones's failure by tossing a few plastic beer bottles towards the ring. One of these hit one of Curry's cornermen. The scenes after Nelson's overwhelming victory were even uglier as a few louts tried to get to Nelson's dressing room and were restrained by the two black American heavyweights, Tim Witherspoon and Sam Scarff. A couple of Nelson's supporters were slightly injured. The situation was quickly contained, but the racial hatred was alarming because all three black champions – Hagler, Curry and Nelson – were clearcut winners and had behaved impeccably in the ring. Unfortunately it only takes a handful of extremists to start a riot. Alcohol plays a major part, as it does with all violence, but banning the sale of it in the arena still does not prevent people tanking up before arriving at the fight.

With all this in mind, there was considerable alarm when West Ham's Mark Kaylor and Errol Christie, a rising black fighter from Coventry, became involved in a brawl at a press luncheon given by Mike Barrett. Mike had signed the two middleweights to meet in a final eliminator for the British middleweight title at Wembley in 1985 and paid £82,000 – a record purse for a non-championship contest in Britain. Some cynics thought the punch-up had been set up to sell more tickets, but there is no doubt this was a genuine row. However, it certainly was not a racial quarrel. Neither fighter referred to the colour of the other's skin but one newspaper was determined to splash it on the front page as a racial brawl with demands to ban the fight for the fear of a Bonfire Night race riot at or around Wembley.

The police, the Boxing Board and Mike Barrett were worried. The promoter arranged for another press gathering for Kaylor and Christie to shake hands and reaffirm that the punch-up had nothing to do with racial differences. Barrett assured the

Board there would be a ban on the sale of alcohol at Wembley. There would be no fanfare of trumpets and both boxers would come into the ring together to avoid stirring up the fans. Extra police and stewards would be present and nobody without authority would be allowed to approach ringside.

Despite continued warnings from the media about possible trouble between West Ham and Coventry fans, the fight went on without any serious incident and turned out to be the best British fight of 1985. It was conducted in a sporting but ferocious manner. Christie was knocked down and hurt almost immediately, but recovered to put Kaylor down before the end of the first round. Kaylor was down again in the third session but by sheer guts forced the pace and knocked out Christie in the eighth round. It was a terrific fight. Unfortunately for Mike Barrett, the riot stories had frightened many regulars away and Wembley was less than three-quarters full. Without the scare stories the promoter would surely have had a sellout.

Kaylor and Christie made many new friends by their splendid performance but they were ordered to appear before the stewards to explain their behaviour, which had brought boxing into disrepute. Kaylor took the blame for throwing a punch following the scuffle outside the press luncheon. The stewards weighed up the evidence for an hour and decided to fine Kaylor £15,000 of his £49,500 purse and Christie £5000 of his £33,000 share. Both boxers and their managers seemed stunned by the amount and appealed against the fines which were considerably reduced by the stewards of appeal.

The next ugly outburst of hooliganism came during the Bruno–Witherspoon world title slam at Wembley Stadium. To suit American television, the contest did not commence until one o'clock on a Sunday morning. This allowed a small minority of the 50,000 crowd to cause havoc. Some arrived from the pubs well tanked up and running battles ensued. A crowd of yobs without tickets ranging from £25 to £150 tried to smash their way past barriers into the vast stadium while others attempted to storm the dearer seats.

We again had the shame of British riff-raff jeering the US national anthem and, worst of all, some 200 chairs plus showers of coins were hurled towards Witherspoon, who had fought a perfectly clean fight. As he left the ring, with his world championship intact, scores of drunken, biased bums chanted 'Rule Britannia'. Others charged towards the ring to attack Witherspoon, who must have an uneasy opinion of the sportsmanship of British fans, recalling how he had a year earlier gone to the assistance of Azumah Nelson in Birmingham after the Ghanian had flattened Cowdell in the first round.

Twenty-seven arrests were made at Wembley and ten police officers were slightly injured. It took only a comparative few yobs to make any top American and foreign fighter fear appearing in England. Alcohol is, of course, partly to blame, but if contests are staged after the pubs are shut it is difficult to stop fans arriving tanked up. British sports fans used to be patronisingly referred to as the best losers in the world; we have now become the worst losers, due to a minority of hooligans infiltrating great sporting events and looking for trouble.

It is a credit to the influence of Barry McGuigan that in Belfast, where religious prejudice is overwhelming, Catholic can box Protestant or black oppose white without rioting within the King's Hall. This arena in the old days was considered pretty tough for a visiting fighter. One of the worst riots took place in 1956. Billy Spider Kelly was defending the British featherweight championship against Charlie Hill from Scotland. When the decision went to Hill the trouble started. It began with booing from the packed hall and then a few wild men began tossing bottles and chairs. Officials and writers disappeared under the ring as missiles crashed into the ring. It was worse than the Hagler–Minter affair, but the crowd's anger was not vented against the winner. The bottles and chairs were thrown after the boxers had left the ring and the violence was not of a racial or religious nature. The crowd were certain that their local hero had done enough to keep the title.

I have found Northern Irish fans to be splendid sportsmen. It does not matter whether a boxer or footballer comes from Dublin or Belfast. To them he is an Irishman, regardless of religion, and they are behind him to a man. Yet I must confess in the days of some tremendous Belfast fighters like Rinty Monaghan, Bunty Doran, John Kelly, Billy Spider Kelly (and his dad Jim Spider Kelly, who also held the British featherweight title), Jimmy Brown, John Caldwell, Freddie Gilroy and many more, I found the huge crowds intimidating.

With the Northern Irish crowd roaring and a heavy contingent of the Ulster Constabulary, the atmosphere seemed unusually tense.

Belfast fans are great partisans. Poor Jimmy Wilde, one of the great flyweight champions, did not qualify as a diplomat. After Monaghan had stopped Jackie Paterson to become world champion, Wilde was invited into the ring to say a few words of congratulations. Jimmy unwisely expressed the opinion that he could have beaten them both in the same ring the same night! He was booed and pelted and the promoter banned Jimmy from the King's Hall for ever!

When Terry Allen, the Londoner, went to the King's Hall to face Rinty for the world title, the atmosphere was unbearably tense, as the referee, Sam Russell, also from London, agreed. Sam, who had also been a matchmaker and manager, was a tremendous character and spent most days at the race track. He admitted to me before the big fight that he could think of better places to be than King's Hall that night, 'especially if Allen turns out to be the winner'. The hall was jammed tight and during a preliminary bout between Bunty Doran and Danny O'Sullivan from London there was a loud bang. Everybody jumped and looked uneasy. A rumour went round that a shot had been fired. It was not until later that we were assured it was a firework that had exploded.

The Monaghan–Allen affair was disappointing but very close. I thought Rinty had just about scraped home but Sam gave a draw. The decision was received in virtual silence. I expected a storm of protest from the Belfast crowd. Perhaps the fact that the title remained with Rinty prevented any trouble. At a party in the Royal Avenue Hotel later I said to Sam, 'You've made history. That's the first time a world title has ended in a draw in Britain.' Russell grinned and wisecracked, 'I was sure that was a gunshot during the Doran–Sullivan fight and I thought of my wife Rosie. She's too young to be a widow!'

The Drug Menace

History shows that the human race does not learn from the failure and disasters of its ancestors. Drugs played a part in the destruction of ancient Greece and the decline and fall of the Roman Empire. Now, some thousands of years later, drugs are an increasing menace to civilization in the twentieth century, not only in the Third World but in the two most powerful of the advanced countries, the United States of America and Soviet Russia, as well as throughout Asia, Africa, Australasia, Europe and South America. Young people never believe that the kind of disasters that destroyed perhaps their fathers or grandfathers will ever hit them. The National Institute of Drug Abuse estimated that some 20 million Americans use marijuana, some 4 million take cocaine and some 2 million are hooked on stimulants.

Drugs have always been used in sport. They were one of the evils that helped end the original Olympic Games. They crept into American boxing years ago when used by unscrupulous fight racketeers to get a boxer beaten. But with scientific advancement most of the drugs used in big sport today are stimulants taken to improve rather than deter performance.

Luckily there is little evidence of drug abuse in British boxing but the BBBC is aware that some American, Mexican and Third World boxers do use stimulants and a system of random tests has been introduced to combat this. The only way to be sure that a boxer has not taken a stimulant is to insist on a urine test before and after each contest. In the old days medical examination of boxers at the weigh-in revealed little. The doctor used his stethoscope to test heart, lungs and not much else.

Although there is not a serious drug problem in boxing in Britain or Europe, it would be unwise to dismiss the menace of drugs in world boxing. Many boxers have risen from poverty, and some from the Third World do not regard drugs as any more dangerous than alcohol. They might well have started the habit before becoming established as fighters. Other fighters have turned to drugs in retirement. Pinklon Thomas, former WBC heavyweight champion, admitted that as a youngster he used to sniff cocaine and had attended a detoxification centre. And Tim Witherspoon, who lost the WBC title to Thomas in 1984 and won the WBA championship from Tony Tubbs in 1986, was found to have used marijuana when tested after the Tubbs fight. He admitted he had smoked it at a party six weeks before the fight. The WBA ordered a rematch between Witherspoon and Tubbs, but Tubbs agreed to British heavyweight Frank Bruno having a title crack at Witherspoon first. Larry Holmes said he tried cocaine once at the age of seventeen but not since.

Even great champions like Alexis Arguello dabbled with cocaine. As did John Conteh. Aaron Pryor, who ended Arguello's career, twice knocking him out in title fights, was reckoned to be the greatest junior welterweight champion and was undefeated in 36 contests. He suddenly went downhill and announced his retirement as WBA champion after beating Arguello a second time. Pryor denied that he had taken drugs. Friends said his problem was one of acute depression and not drugs. But the IBF stripped him of his title because of his inactivity over a nine-month period. He had announced his retirement after beating Arguello for the second time in September 1983, and though he spent months training in a gymnasium in 1985, he did not take part in another contest that year.

In September 1985 the New Jersey Athletic Commission suspended thirty-nine professional boxers for ninety days. These suspensions were subsequently lifted, samples having been taken eight months after positive testing. The Commission is mainly seeking to detect marijuana, cocaine, heroin and any stimulants. It intends to continue drug testing and is aiming to speed up the procedure.

In some cases boxers claim that they have used drugs such as Ephedrine to free a blocked-up nose. The Michigan Commission ruled a fight for the USBA bantam title between Freddie Jackson and Hurley Snead to be no contest after Jackson had been awarded a split decision when traces of marijuana were found in his system. The championship was returned to Snead.

Livingston Bramble, from New Jersey, failed a test after retaining the WBA lightweight title against Ray Mancini at Reno in 1985. The Nevada Commission found a trace of Ephedrine in a post-fight test. Mancini's manager, David Wolf, called on the WBA to overturn the decision, but Bramble's claim that he had inhaled some Ephedrine to clear a stuffy nose a day or so before the fight was upheld and the decision stood.

Azumah Nelson was cleared of using illegal drugs after retaining the WBC featherweight title against Marcos Villasana. The WBC claim they have carried out more than four hundred post-fight urine tests in a decade without any serious positive findings.

Worldwide drugs have played a bigger part in athletics, American football and baseball and soccer than they have in boxing. American, Soviet and other Eastern Bloc officials have turned a blind eye to the use of stimulants and muscle-building steroids for many years. When an army of athletes of all nations meet in an Olympic village they swap views and ideas. The big topic at the Mexico Olympics of 1968 was steroids. The practice is on the increase. The world of cricket was rocked in 1986 when Ian Botham, the tremendous all-rounder, confessed after repeated denials that he had at various times in the past smoked pot. And dope tests are made in the World Snooker championships.

Two men who for many years fought the good fight against drug abuse in sport are Professor Arnold Beckett and Sir Arthur Gold. I recall talking at length to Professor Beckett, a member of the Olympic Health Committee, at the Chelsea Drug Centre after the Moscow Olympics in 1980. He had been unhappy about the drug control at the Games and warned that unless we can change the belief of our young people that to compete successfully against the rest of the world in sport they must resort to drugs, there will be a serious deterioration in their health. On the subject of anabolic steroids he said, 'Men and women continually using them take as big a risk of liver cancer as the habitual smoker does of developing lung cancer. They can also cause jaundice, fluid retention and psychological and personality changes.' Sir Arthur Gold, as president of the European Athletic Association, told me, 'The use of drugs in sport is far more rife than people care to admit. Some youngsters would sell their souls for success and I'm afraid there is an unhealthy and dishonest approach by some of the world's greatest athletes. The only way it can be stopped is by consistent random tests.'

Crusaders like Professor Beckett and Sir Arthur genuinely have the health of young people at heart, realizing that sporting success through drugs can bring misery before middle age. But, alas, there are not enough people like them. Drugs were used at the Los Angeles Olympics in 1984 and will be used again in South Korea in 1988. They are part of any sport in which prize money or appearance money can make youngsters millionaires while still in their twenties. It has happened in snooker: Kirk Stevens, the young Canadian, admitted taking them, though not before a match. In 1985 the Men's Professional Council, the governing body of world tennis, approved a rule making all players liable to random drug tests from 1986. This applies to Wimbledon, the American, French, Australian championships and to other major tournaments. Even the English Ladies' Golf Association, which is fairly certain that it has no drug problem, agreed in 1985 to cooperate with the Sports Council's campaign to rid sport of drug abuse.

All controlling sports bodies must be alert. If unchecked, drug taking could develop into the ugliest of all sporting calamities. Surely there can be few more evil men than those who push drugs for financial gain, knowing they are destroying the lives of young people whether they be potential sporting champions or just mixed-up kids. It is a double tragedy when superbly fit athletes use stimulants. There is always the danger they may get hooked.

BOOK FOUR

THE AGONY

Three Tragic Worldbeaters

Between July 1965 and November 1966 three of Britain's most successful post-war boxers, all former world champions, died violently. In sixteen traumatic months Freddie Mills and Randolph Turpin committed suicide, and Jackie Paterson was killed in a drunken brawl in South Africa.

In the early hours of the morning of 25 July 1965 a broad-shouldered man with a mop of thick black hair was found slumped in the back of his car in an alley in Soho. A rifle, the type used in fairgrounds, was also in the car. Two tiny .22 bullets had been fired. The man had been shot through his right eye and was dead.

On reading the morning papers, the whole country was shocked to learn that Freddie Mills had committed suicide. He was forty-six. The car had been parked, as usual, in a derelict yard behind Freddie Mills Nite Spot, the club he owned with partner Andy Ho. The young doorman of the club, who first found him, a waiter, Andy Ho and later Mills's wife Chrissie were horrified that Freddie, who had gone to the car for a sleep before midnight, was already dead. Chrissie and Donnie, her son by her first marriage to the South African heavyweight Don McCorkindale, do not accept that he took his own life and are still convinced he was the victim of a gangland murder.

The police and the Westminster coroner were satisfied that it was a case of suicide. Yet more than twenty years after his death the rumour that Freddie Mills was murdered occasionally crops up. I have no wish to reopen the controversy which some newspapers and magazines revive from time to time. The Freddie Mills whom I first met in 1939 was a most happy fellow. He had a lovely smile and was the last man one would connect with suicide. There is no doubt that he changed a great deal in the few years before his death. He suffered from depression after the failure of several businesses, including a short spell as a promoter. His club, which he had opened so optimistically as a Chinese restaurant in 1946, had become a financial disaster as a night club and an embarrassment after sordid publicity in a Sunday paper. He had lost the £100,000 he had grossed from boxing and was increasingly troubled by headaches.

He had first suffered from headaches after the thrashing he took in his first world title bid against Gus Lesnevich in 1946. His memory began to fade a little. He had been a fairly regular guest of mine at the Boxing Writers' Club annual dinner but did not arrive one year in the early sixties. I rang next day to inquire what had happened and an embarrassed Freddie apologized, admitting he had completely forgotten the date. It had never happened before. My own view, and I stress this is only an opinion with no fresh evidence, is that, with all his financial problems, the decline of his club and newspaper reports that some of the girl hostesses were prostitutes, everything became too much for him, he suffered terrible depression and took his own life with the rifle which he had borrowed from a friend at Battersea fairground.

There was no question of Freddie Mills being punch-drunk but there is no doubt that he absorbed too much punishment in a short time. He was rushed into the first Lesnevich fight against his better judgement. He had not readjusted after a year in India with the RAF and had been troubled by a blood disorder. He was discharged early in 1946 but would have preferred a few more months before tackling Lesnevich at Harringay on 14 May and Bruce Woodcock on 4 June. Jack Solomons was anxious to get off to a post-war boxing boom at Harringay. Mills got tagged in the second round and was smashed to the canvas three times. He made an extraordinary comeback and was actually ahead when he was tagged again and stopped in round 10. Three weeks later he was back in the same ring for a punishing twelve rounds against the heavyweight champion Woodcock and was beaten on points. The following November he was tossed in against Joe Baksi. Poor Freddie was getting the stuffing knocked out of him. Yet he was still a tremendous light-heavyweight: he took the world title from Lesnevich in 1948, but lost it to Joey Maxim in 1950.

Freddie Mills should have enjoyed his hard-earned cash during the next fifteen years, but it was not to be. About a thousand mourners packed into or around St Giles Parish Church, Camberwell, with hundreds more lining the streets for his funeral. The final curtain should never have fallen on this nice guy's life at forty-six.

Less than a year after they buried Freddie Mills there was more heartbreaking news that Randolph Turpin, who had brought pride to Britain in 1951 by defeating the incomparable Sugar Ray Robinson, had shot himself. He had not reached his thirty-eighth birthday. On 17 May 1966 Turpin kissed two of his daughters, Gwyneth and Annette, goodbye as they returned to school after lunch and went upstairs to a bedroom on the first floor of Gwyn's Transport Cafe in Leamington, which was run by his wife with Randolph doing the cooking. He was checking on his third daughter, Charmaine, who was in bed with a cold. When he did not return Gwen went to see where he was and was shocked to find her husband slumped by a bed on which Carmen, their twenty-month-old baby was sitting crying with blood on her face. Gwen rushed to a nearby hospital carrying the baby, who had a bullet in her head and another in her chest. The child was detained in hospital for three weeks. Turpin was dead.

Unlike Mills, Randolph had never in his younger days given me the impression he had a sense of fun. Ironically, he would have been better off if he had never become a world champion caught up with the glamour of New York, collecting a number of fair-weather friends. He was unable to handle or keep the fortune he earned with his two fists. He was physically strong with a weak character, a simple lad who was not equipped to cope with the situation he suddenly found himself tossed into. He had been modest up to the Robinson victory, but his behaviour before his American fights against Robinson in 1951 and against Bobo Olson two years later was eccentric and irresponsible. He set up camp at Grossinger's in the Catskill Mountains, some 120 miles from New York City, and led all of us who were in America to report his chances a merry old dance. For the Olson fight he took over from his manager, quarrelled with his brother Dick, a former British champion, and continually broke training.

Many unpleasant rumours were floating around that he was having a good time with Adele Daniels, a pretty black girl he had met at the time of the second Robinson fight. Randolph showed little sense of responsibility or ambition, considering this was his chance to regain the world title. I recall meeting Harry Markson, of the International Boxing Club, at the entrance to Madison Square Garden an hour before the fight. He had just given permission for one of Turpin's seconds to go outside and buy some comics. Harry was greatly amused. 'Can't your guy read?' he asked, 'He only looks at comics.'

Turpin's performance was disappointing. Olson was not in the same class as Robinson, but after boxing well for three rounds the British fighter changed his tactics and kept leaning back on the ropes, allowing Olson to hit him. He took counts in rounds 9 and 10 and was well beaten on points. He had fought a brainless fight and was only a shadow of the fighter who had twice faced Robinson two years earlier. He did not show any regret or concern that he had thrown away the chance of becoming champion again.

The day he was due to sail home on the *Queen Mary*, Randolph was arrested by New York police, taken to court and charged with assaulting Adele Daniels. Miss Daniels withdrew charges but said she would sue him for $100,000. He was allowed to return to Britain but had to leave $10,000 as security. She later filed a law suit for rape and assault. Turpin did not return to New York until 1955. After a bizarre court case lasting nearly a week Miss Daniels settled for around $3000.

After the Olson fight Turpin, divorced from his first wife, married Gwen Price, a Welsh girl, and seemed happy with her and their four daughters. His boxing career became completely erratic. He was knocked out in one round by Tiberio Mitri in Rome to lose the European title and flattened in four rounds by the Canadian Gordon Wallace. Yet he twice halted Alex Buxton in British light-heavyweight championship bouts to win a

Lonsdale Belt outright and outpointed Arthur Howard before relinquishing this title. He was knocked out by Yolande Pompey in two rounds in 1958 and then retired. Three years later he took up all-in wrestling. Like many ex-champions, he was found to have heavy tax debts. He had grossed perhaps £300,000 from his seventy-three contests – over £60,000 from the second Robinson bout – but it had all gone. A hotel bought in partnership with a business contact had been sold. Turpin was in one hell of a mess financially. He was declared bankrupt, the tax people were still chasing him and his cafe was needed for a car park by the local council.

Turpin was only really happy with the simple things. He blamed many people for his terrible financial plight but did not help himself. He could not handle money, he acted stupidly and brought much misery on himself but, poor fellow, he paid for it with his own life, at thirty-seven.

Do not blame his tragic death on boxing. As an eighteen-year-old assistant cook in the navy he had been charged with attempted suicide, having taken an overdose following a quarrel with his girl. He had so much boxing ability but so little stability. He was not born to be a survivor.

Six months after Turpin's suicide a third former British world champion died violently. Jackie Paterson, the hardest-hitting flyweight since Benny Lynch, was jabbed in the throat with a broken bottle in a drunken brawl. The Scot was working as a truck driver at Durban and became involved in a stupid argument at Amanzimtoti on the coast over the names and whereabouts of certain streets in England. Alcohol and adrenalin flowed. Tempers were lost. Jackie Paterson died at forty-six.

The tragedy was that, at the age of twenty-six and having been a professional for eight years, he held five major titles – world, British and Empire flyweight and British and Empire bantam crowns; he also held the European bantam championship for a few months and seemed set up financially for life.

He had been lucky to have married Helen, a schoolgirl sweetheart, with a good business sense, who handled their finances; at one time they had £100,000 in the bank and bought three fruit shops. I visited their home in Glasgow and travelled with them to Paris in 1945 when Jackie fought Theo Medina. If any champion, I thought, was made for life, it was Jackie Paterson. At this time he was a strict teetotaller and non-smoker and not interested in gambling. Then suddenly everything went wrong when friends took him greyhound racing. After beginner's luck when he won a small fortune, he turned out to be a compulsive gambler and could not stop. He never told Helen of his visits to Shawfield and Albion dog tracks, and when the winnings turned to heavy losses he began writing large cheques. A terrible row followed. In four years he had not only lost the £25,000 he estimated he had won but a further £55,000, and when the tax man caught up with him to demand nearly £8000 unpaid surtax for earnings between 1943 and 1948, the Patersons had to sell the shops, two cars and three vans. He was declared bankrupt.

Coinciding with his gambling sprees he put on weight, which cost him three flyweight titles when facing Rinty Monaghan at Belfast in 1948. He spent the night before the fight wrapped in heavy sweaters sitting in front of a boiler in the basement of his house, sweating off pounds. Stories broke that he could not be found and the fight was off but he turned up for the weigh-in, only just made 8 stone, but was so weak that it was surprising the fight lasted even seven rounds. At this stage he was gambling but had not yet got into heavy debt.

But the worst was yet to come. Helen stood by him after he went bankrupt and he took a job running a bar at Largs in Ayrshire without a salary because it provided accommodation for Helen, himself and their two sons. It was while running the bar that he met a man who reckoned he could get him a job as a trainee manager at a hotel in South Africa. The idea of starting all over again in a new country appealed to the Scot and the Patersons emigrated in 1954. But it did not work out; after starting well working as a barman, manager and insurance salesman, Jackie began drinking heavily and collected a bunch of friends who encouraged him to drink more and more. He became quarrelsome and, after insulting the hotel owner and his wife, was sacked. Jackie went on regular benders and his marriage ended.

Though Helen divorced him, she gave him £1000 to return to Britain and saw him off at the airport. But Jackie was set on the road to ruin with old drinking friends in London and Glasgow.

The £1000 was soon spent and he worked as a barman in a dozen pubs. He also tried his hand as a wine bottler, paper packer, groundsman, stoker for the Gas Board, in a crucible works and a plant-hire firm. Despite all the bad years and hoping desperately for a reconciliation, he had kept in touch with Helen, who was working for Jackie's old boss in South Africa. He returned to South Africa and got himself a job driving a truck, but he could not stop drinking. It was during a boozing session at the seaside town of Amanzimtoti that the stupid argument began and the life of the man, who had taken part in ninety-two professional fights including twelve championships and was world champion for five years, was so cheaply thrown away.

Let us spare a thought for the agony Freddie Mills, Randolph Turpin and Jackie Paterson and their families went through and remember that, though in the end their lives were wasted, each was an outstanding champion who had brought glory to Britain.

Skid Row

It was the most depressing day of his life on a cold morning in January 1949. The tubby thirty-seven-year-old man with scarred eyebrows woke up in the drunk section cell of a Los Angeles police station. He was still hung over from a drunken night on the town. Looking around at the other vagrants and alcoholics, he shuddered as the happenings of the night before came slowly back like a horrendous nightmare. He had wrapped his yellow convertible round a lamppost and had resisted arrest when two cops found him. Could this bum be Henry Armstrong, the only man to hold three world boxing titles at the same time? He had reached rock bottom and was ashamed.

It had begun like so many nights of recent years. First one bar and then another, drinking whisky and talking about the good days when the world had looked up to him. His two rugged fists had grossed well over half a million bucks and he drove fast cars and escorted fast women. But this time he did not remember leaving the last bar or mounting the kerb and crashing into the lamppost until the police arrested him.

After losing the last of his three titles in 1941 with blood pouring from both eyes and nose, Henry Armstrong had announced his retirement. With much assistance from his old manager, he had blown a fortune, and fighting was all he knew. So he went on throwing and taking punches for his supper for another five years. But he had developed a taste for booze. Eddie Mead had not done him any favours when, in order for Henry to put on weight to bid for the lightweight and welterweight titles, he had encouraged the boxer to drink beer.

From beer Armstrong moved to whisky and thought he was having fun as he drank the nights away. He had become a lush.

Later he was to feel more shame when called before the judge, a woman named Ida Adams. She said quietly, 'Henry Armstrong, what are *you* doing here?' He lowered his head as she continued, 'I reckon you haven't only let yourself down but also a million boys.' She fined him a nominal $10. With head still down, he mumbled his regrets and shuffled from the court, resolved to kick the booze, but drinking is not an easy habit to abandon and, despite his efforts, he still ended up at parties and in bars. As a poor kid he had always loved poetry and had written some crude but sincere verses even when still fighting. One, entitled 'I Meant to Do Good', was a long rambling confession of his own frailties and revealed he had a conscience. Each verse ended with the line 'I meant to do Good'.

Then one night he had a vivid dream. He saw himself in the middle of the Los Angeles Coliseum. The audience was not boxing fans but thousands of men, women and children. They were praying and singing. He woke and fell out of bed. He felt he wanted to preach and picked up a bible, which he had not read for years. That night he turned his back on alcohol.

After the dream, which he insists was a miracle, his desire to become a preacher was realized when a blind Negro Baptist minister invited him to address an audience at his church in Pasadena. He was ordained a few years later and was received with warm affection by his congregation. This gave him more pleasure than the roar of the crowd when he was a triple champion and he sensed an inner calm he had never known before. He was only forty-one but figured he had journeyed to Hell and back. Henry Armstrong had found peace at last.

The Shame of a Brave Man

What is more distressing than seeing a brave man quit cold? A 25,000 crowd in the Superdrome in New Orleans and many millions on world television could not believe their eyes. Roberto Duran, a man of red blood and guts, waved a glove in frustration and shouted, '*No mas! No mas!*' as he quit in less than eight bloodless rounds. He had surrendered the world welterweight championship to Sugar Ray Leonard. It was an incredible sight.

He had inflicted the only defeat on Leonard a few months earlier, demonstrating that the once great lightweight was now the invisible welterweight. Yet now he capitulated without taking a really vicious punch or spilling a drop of blood. The bemused referee glanced at him appealingly. 'Why? Why?' The crowd, including fans who had flown in from Panama City, were stunned to silence. A knockout defeat would have been honourable. Instead, they had witnessed the assassination of a national hero. The whole of Panama was in mourning.

Why? This Man of Stone had lost only one decision in seventy-three bouts and had never been stopped. Why had he abdicated his priceless crown so pathetically? Was it a fix for a betting coup? Was it because of stomach cramps, as the fallen hero claimed later? Neither excuse made sense.

The truth was that the morale of the toughest and roughest fighter in years had cracked when Leonard, having learned by the mistakes of the first contest, decided to dazzle and humiliate El Animal by sheer speed and science. With Angelo Dundee advising him in his corner, he danced, taunted and tormented the savage Latin with all the ruthlessness and class of Ali himself. In a bar brawl Duran would take on all-comers all night, but in a ring, without getting hurt, his mercurial temperament could not take public ridicule. It was his pride and not his body that was wounded. He was demoralized and frustrated in round 8 when his tormentor almost did a tap dance, dropped his arms, stuck out his chin to be hit and then stuck out his tongue, holding his opponent in complete contempt as Ali had done with British champion Richard Dunn at Munich four years earlier.

For Leonard it was sweet revenge. Duran had declined to shake hands after the first fight, and now, with controlled arrogance, Sugar Ray declared, 'To make any man quit is an achievement. To make Roberto Duran quit seemed impossible. It was better than knocking him out. I outclassed, humiliated and frustrated him. He couldn't take it mentally. I didn't hurt him or make him bleed. I just made him look a fool before millions.'

No one was more shattered than the veteran trainers Freddie Brown and Ray Arcel when Roberto suddenly stopped boxing, shook a glove in Leonard's direction, cried *'No mas!'* and turned his back and walked to his corner. Arcel, then eighty-one, growled, 'Now I've seen everything. If any guy had told me Duran even knew how to quit I'd have spat in his eyes.'

There were rumours that Duran had held a party after the debacle and was heard singing with his wife, and that he ate and drank a lot. If true, that belies his excuse of stomach cramp. I dismiss the inevitable cries of fix because a true fix would have been stage-managed: there was no way that Duran would have agreed to give the impression he was a coward. The Louisiana State Commission fined him $6000 – a joke, as $4 million had already been deposited in a bank in Panama City.

He hid from the boxing public for six months. His shame was great and so was his penance, but he was determined to convince the people of Panama and of the United States that he was not chicken and that brave men do not really quit.

Happily, Duran lived to fight another day and to prove to the world he was as brave as he was great. Less than three years after the ignominy of the second Leonard fight, he shook the boxing fraternity by knocking out Davey Moore to win the world junior middleweight crown – his third world title. A few months later he took Marvin Hagler fifteen rounds in a gutsy attempt to win the middleweight championship. He had indeed vindicated himself after the stigma of New Orleans.

The Greek God

We were gathered at the old Jack of Clubs in Soho. Our chief guest was Max Baer, former world heavyweight champion and such a character that he was known as the Clown Prince of boxing. It was 1958 and Baer, long retired, was still a magnificent giant of a man with greying hair, a little more subdued than the playboy of the thirties who had come to London to face Tommy Farr and Ben Foord. He had been invited back to England by Jack Solomons for a night of nostalgia when the final curtain was to come down on Harringay Arena, which, having staged so many great fights for twenty-two years, was to be sold to become a food warehouse. Among former champions invited were Henry Armstrong, Gus Lesnevich, Rinty Monoghan, Randolph Turpin, Tommy Farr, Eric Boon, Arthur Danahar, Ernie Roderick, Freddie Mills, Bruce Woodcock, Don Cockell, Johnny Williams, Peter Kane and there were many more who had helped to make the famous arena vibrate.

As we sat eating, my thoughts went back to 1936 and Harringay's first ever fight between Ben Foord, the South African who had won the British heavyweight title from Jack Petersen and Walter Neusel, the German who had twice beaten Petersen at Wembley. Harringay was the perfect arena for boxing. Built in a circle like the old Blackfriars Ring but on luxurious lines, there was not a bad seat in the house. In 1937, after Farr had taken the title off Foord, Hulls signed Baer to meet the Welshman. Maxie was a tremendous personality from the world of showbiz. He had gone to Hollywood to star in a film *The Prizefighter and the Lady*. Primo Carnera, the official champion, had been hired to take part in the film with glamour boy Baer holding him to a draw. There were weeks of rehearsals and Baer used the time to study the clumsy Italian's every move. When they met for real with the title at stake Maxie knew all the answers. He knocked Carnera down in each of the eleven rounds the fight lasted and was crowned champion. Baer, like Ali later, used to bait his opponents. At the weigh-in he had the onlookers laughing at Carnera as he pretended to pluck hairs from Primo's chest, reciting, 'He loves me. He loves me not!' And when the giant tripped over Baer's foot in the second round and they both went down, Baer wisecracked, 'Come on, Primo. Last one up is a cissy!'

Baer was born in Omaha, Nebraska. His father was a German Jew and his mother had Scottish blood. Though a playboy he won seventy of eighty-three bouts and knocked out tough fighters like Schmeling and Galento. Yet he flopped badly against Louis and was twice battered by Lou Nova. He blew the title clowning against Jim Braddock, a 10-1 underdog, and played around in London before Farr gave him a good beating over twelve rounds, but he beat Tommy over fifteen rounds in New York.

The lunch was nearly over, the coffee served and Maxie, all 6 ft 2 in of him, rose to speak. It was all too brief. 'You guys were great to me when I was here to fight Farr,' he said. 'I had a ball in London. You all treated me swell and I want to thank you for treating me swell again.' He stopped talking, fumbled in his pockets for a handkerchief and burst into tears. There was an embarrassing silence as he sobbed before apologizing. Then he added, 'One of you guys described me as a Greek god. Now look at me. I look like a god-damned Greek!'

Lousy Requiem for a Heavyweight

No matter how historians present Sonny Liston – world heavyweight champion, convict and bully – he deserved more out of life. Although a champion, he was a born loser. He was spawned in squalor in Little Rock, Arkansas, one of twenty-five children of a man who served two wives. From his earliest memories he was waging a war of attrition with the cops; he went to reform school, prison and even as champion was controlled by hoodlums. He fought only two men twice each for the title. Against Floyd Patterson he was a gladiator, against Ali a bum. He was the only heavyweight champ never permitted to fight in New York because of his gangster associates.

His death when under forty was as controversial as his four troubled decades on earth. How he died remains unanswered. Did he take an overdose or was he murdered during the last few hours that remained of the year 1970? His gravestone in Paradise Gardens Cemetery, Las Vegas, peacefully away from the vulgarity of the bizarre casinos along the Strip, ignores his eighteen months of brief glory. The curious visitor is informed that beneath it lie the remains of

Charles 'Sonny' Liston
1932–1970
'A Man'

All that can be said is Sonny Liston found a tranquillity in death that escaped him in life. He had been dead twelve years when Shelby Strother, of the *Los Angeles Times*, asked the caretaker of the cemetery where he would find Liston's grave. He was told, 'It's right by the arborvitae bush. Not many people come to see his grave. Usually only other boxers. It's like people have forgotten all about Sonny Liston.' The man from LA added that the marker was rusting and weeds surrounded it. A lousy requiem for a heavyweight.

Yet his funeral on 9 January 1971 was given the pomp of showbiz. Seven hundred mourners, including Joe Louis, Muhammad Ali, Sugar Ray Robinson, Sammy Davis Junior, Doris Day and Ella Fitzgerald were in the procession of limousines with motorcycle escort that went down the Strip and away to Paradise Gardens.

Liston was nearly twenty-eight before he received recognition as a possible contender. He had a bad record with the law, had been in prison and was said to be run by Blinky Palermo in Philadelphia. When he was matched with Floyd Patterson in Chicago in 1962, it turned out to be the biggest massacre since the St Valentine's Day shoot-up. Liston intimidated Patterson at the weigh-in and again before the first bell. Floyd was flattened in the first round and afterwards slipped out of Chicago in disguise wearing a false beard. Ten months later Liston again destroyed Patterson in a couple of minutes at Las Vegas and the monster legend was born. Yet within six months the X certificate was lifted when a brash twenty-two-year-old Cassius Clay II presented him as quitter and at the second attempt destroyed him as a fighter of credibility for ever, with one punch.

He did not fight again for a year. After winning a few unimportant bouts in Sweden, he took part in uneventful contests around America and in 1969 was matched with Leotis Martin in Las Vegas but was knocked out in nine rounds. He had one more try, stopping the much battered Chuck Wepner in the summer of 1970. He had little ambition left but loved gambling in downtown Las Vegas. Then, on New Year's Eve, while the crowds were celebrating, Sonny Liston died alone in his flat. His wife Geraldine and adopted son Danille were visiting her sick father in St Louis.

His body was found five or six days later. There were needle pricks in his arms and death was assumed to be from an overdose of heroin, but his wife and some close associates dismissed the suggestion of suicide. The coroner's finding was heart failure. Harold Conrad, a good newspaper man and later a first-class fight publicist who handled many Ali and Liston fights, reckoned he was murdered. Conrad wrote, 'Liston was scared of needles. He went down with flu before the second Ali fight but when the doctor suggested a jab, he wanted to throw the doc out of the window. Out of training he drank heavily and heroin isn't in a boozer's bag. He smoked a little pot and did a little snorting but never went for hard drugs. He knocked around with some bad guys and put pressure on them when drunk. After he got stinking one night they took him home, jabbed him an OD and that's the end of Sonny.' Conrad added, 'I talked to a guy in the Vegas sheriff's office who said, "A bad nigger. He got what was coming to him." But I don't buy that. He had some good qualities, but I think he died the day before he was born.'

I once had an exclusive interview with Liston in America before he was champion. I could only get a 'Yeah' or a 'No' out of him. He was sullen, intimidating, but one had to allow for his upbringing and lack of education. He could not read or write and had some bad acquaintances. He trusted few adults, black or white, but could be relaxed when he had kids around him. Was he a drug addict at the end, or did his heart just give up, or was he murdered? Sonny took the truth with him to the grave. He was a born loser and Harold Conrad said it all: 'He died the day before he was born.'

His Own Executioner

I can think of few more distressing scenes than being witness to the destruction and humiliation of a super-champion, and more so if it is self-destruction. The third of October 1938 was a macabre night at the Empress Hall, Earl's Court. We had seen the rapid decline of Benny Lynch and now we were gathered at the National Sporting Club tournament for the inevitable final fall of a wonderful but wayward champion.

The record book will tell you that wee Benny was knocked out in three rounds for the only time in his career of over a hundred contests. His opponent was Aurel Toma, a moderate Rumanian bantam whose only claim to fame was that he had once been a chauffeur to King Carol, the deposed ruler of his country. Poor Benny was certainly counted out, but if ever there was a self-inflicted KO this was it. He had been on the booze for days and climbed into the ring with one big hangover. How he was allowed to box remains a mystery. After losing his world crown through lack of condition that June, he had been fined £200 by the Boxing Board. Only five nights before he met Toma he had been fined a further £500 for failing to make even 8 st 10 lb against an American fighter, K. O. Morgan, and was beaten on points. He had also promised Jack Harding, the general manager of the NSC, to make 8 st 10 lb against Toma, but Harding could not contact Benny the night before the fight. He was eventually traced to a house, and was found nursing a bottle of Scotch and a packet of cigarettes. He was taken to a Turkish bath and sobered up; at the weigh-in he scaled 9 st $5\frac{1}{4}$ lb but was passed as medically fit. By that evening he was far from fit. He clearly had been drinking again and was actually smoking a cigarette in the dressing room. When he climbed into the ring his performance was catastrophic. The man who was world champion four months earlier could not even go through the motions from memory. He was slow, flat-footed and minus his uncanny timing and stamina. Yet, fighting in this half world, he was still brave and stumbled forward, missing more punches than he landed. Toma could see Benny was unable to fight and did not try to defend. The crowd began the cruel slow handclap and the farce which had become a tragedy ended when Benny fell flat in round 3 and was counted out.

Benny had very few true friends, but one was Johnny McGrory, former British featherweight, who had first met him at Sammy Wilson's gym. Johnny arranged for Benny to visit Mellaray Monastery, a home for alcoholics 140 miles from Dublin. But Benny could not stand the discipline and returned to Scotland. The NSC then arranged for him to go into a nursing home at Chislehurst in Kent but, on hearing one of his sons, Bobby, was ill, he hurried back to Glasgow. Benny made one last attempt to kick alcohol. He accepted a fight in Swansea and went into vigorous training, but again he slipped and was found, clad in pyjamas, unconscious on a Scottish moor. The Boxing Board ordered a physical check-up; Benny was found to have heart trouble and his licence was withdrawn. Almost down and out, he returned to the boxing booths which had helped build him up eight years earlier.

He was living alone in a room in Glasgow when on 8 August 1946 in terrible health he walked into a hospital and died a few hours later. He was thirty-three. Scotland was shocked and an estimated 3000 lined the streets or followed the coffin to St Kentigern's Cemetery. His friends erected a stone for his grave bearing the simple words: 'Always a fighter'. Nearly forty years have passed and Scotland has not forgotten its greatest pugilist. A new headstone has been erected with a figure of Benny inscribed and 'Always a fighter' renewed in gold letters.

Benny Lynch was a victim of human frailty, unable to cope with the fame his great talent brought him. He had been brought up in the back streets of the Gorbals which seldom enjoyed the luxury of free sunshine. He was brought up in a one-room tenement with one bed shared by his mother, father and older brother, who did not even survive to manhood. So let us remember him not for his weakness but for his greatness. No fairer or more sporting boxer entered the ring. Without the bottle he was a kind man, who never had much in life to enjoy and whose glory was too brief. He did little harm to any man, with the exception of a man named Benny Lynch.

Breakfast at Caesar's

I shall always remember breakfast at Caesar's on an October morning in 1980. It is not a happy memory because I was waiting for Joe Louis, then a sick man. Caesar's, of course, is Caesar's Palace in Las Vegas, that bizarre combination of hotel, casino, showbiz and boxing mecca where for twenty-four hours each day the curtains shut out both the bright Nevada sunshine and the moonlight, so that time means nothing to the gamblers. It was the morning after another all-time great, Muhammad Ali, having stayed around too long, had cut a pathetic figure in his bid to win the heavyweight title for a fourth time against Larry Holmes. Time had run out for the Greatest, who now had nothing left. Holmes almost gently ended the challenge after ten rounds. Ali for the first and only time in his career failed to stay for the final bell.

They had wheeled Joe Louis in an invalid chair to ringside where Frank Sinatra was seated. Old Blue Eyes and some casino bosses who had moved from Chicago to Vegas picked up the tab for the old Brown Bomber, now little more than a cabbage following open-heart surgery and psychiatric treatment, and now paralysed after two strokes. It was good at least to know that Joe was taken care of in Vegas in his last days because the $5 million he had grossed before the days of television had long since evaporated, mostly in paying off taxes accumulated when he was king. All that remained was an unequalled record and a wonderful name.

An old New York fight manager from the days of Mike Jacobs was trying to set up benefit nights for Joe in different cities and wanted to include London. He was meeting Joe and his wife at Caesar's and asked me to come along. I hesitated, not because I did not want to assist in any minute way to help that great fighter but, seeing the state of his health, I was worried about intruding. I need not have worried. We waited at a table to which Joe was brought each day. Hundreds were gambling all around with dice, roulette, black jack and one-armed bandits, and though the electric lights were on, it seemed more like midnight than breakfast time.

The Brown Bomber was wheeled in by his wife and a woman friend. Poor Joe was helpless and I do not think his wife was pleased to see either of us, but my visit was made worthwhile when the old champion looked up, made gurgling noises and his eyes lit up. 'Joe recognizes you,' his wife said with delight. It was an emotional moment for I had met him many times when he had been champion and ex-champion. We sat there for a little while talking to his wife while she fed him with a spoon, but I knew that time was running out too fast for Joe to survive many benefit nights. It was sad to realize this sick man was once the most feared gladiator in the world. I placed one hand on a broad shoulder as I said goodbye. I knew it was the last time I would be privileged to be in his company. Six months later I read in London that Joe Louis was dead.

Sweet and Sour

A little Welshman boarded the 1.20 a.m. Cardiff-bound train at Paddington on 24 January 1968 and locked himself in a first-class sleeper compartment. It was the first time in his life that Howard Winstone had travelled first class. The reason for the luxury was that, four hours earlier at the Albert Hall, he had at his fourth attempt won the world featherweight championship, stopping Mitsunori Seki, of Japan, in nine rounds. He wanted to be alone and sort out a recipe life had served him of sweet and sour. Before he faced a triumphant reception from the people of Merthyr he was due at a Cardiff divorce court to end the marriage to his boyhood sweetheart Benita. They had married when she was sixteen and he seventeen. They now had four children, two boys and twin girls. Like all young couples, they believed they would live happily ever after, but such bliss is only guaranteed in fairy stories. He was approaching twenty-nine and had been boxing sixteen years, ten as a professional. His belated triumph had come when his best fighting days were behind him. The three wars against the Mexican champion Saldivar had taken their toll.

He had travelled to London second class and had taken the Underground from his hotel to the Albert Hall. After beating Seki he took his mother and sister and sons Wayne and Roy to celebrate with a meal of egg and chips in a little Italian restaurant in Soho. But the glory as a world champion was all too brief.

A couple of months later in a non-title fight he found himself in the unusual situation of getting knocked down by Jimmy

Anderson and though he climbed up to take the decision, the writing was on the wall. Three months later he lost his world crown when stopped in five rounds at Porthcawl by an opponent far less of an artist but with the decisive advantage of youth, Jose Legra from Cuba. The gallant Welshman never fought again, relinquishing his British title. He had never lost his European crown in the ring either. This had been taken away while he was concentrating on his world title challenges against Saldivar.

Despite his tremendous record and the fact that he grossed around £100,000 over ten years, Howard Winstone was to face some lean years. Heavy taxes took a large slice of his savings. As a boxer Howard Winstone was outstanding. As a businessman he was a failure. He bought and sold a snackbar and a haberdashery and rented a pub at Aberdare, but his savings dwindled and eventually he was broke. His problems were aggravated by a trapped sciatic nerve, which gave him a great deal of trouble in his back. He had married again, to Bronwen, three years after his divorce from Benita, but he still had his children to look after and, with a bad back at a time of heavy unemployment, he was forced to seek public assistance. Sad for the man who had been awarded an MBE and made a Freeman of the Borough of Merthyr.

When he finished boxing he had a bungalow proudly named Lonsdale. He reckoned he had paid £40,000 in taxes and figured he could live modestly but comfortably with a few thousand in the bank. Then he found he still owed tax so, to settle up, he sold his bungalow and moved into a terraced house in Merthyr. Despite the hard times, Howard Winstone retained his pride and declined to sell the two Lonsdale Belts he had won outright or his world championship trophy.

It is easy for an ex-fighter out of work to go all the way downhill, but Howard Winstone, despite some depressing years when he feared the worst, has kept going and looked a proud and happy man when the British Boxing Board invited him to London in 1985 to present the British Boxer of the Year award to Barry McGuigan. McGuigan had won the world featherweight title, which only Howard Winstone and one other Briton, Jim Driscoll, back in 1909, had held in nearly a hundred years of that division's history. And, with all his bad luck, Howard was more fortunate than his three-times conqueror. Vincente Saldivar, renowned for his fitness, strength and stamina, died of a heart attack in July 1985. He was only forty-two.

Nobbins for a Champ

It was to have been a social occasion for me at the Cafe Royal on 25 January 1982. The National Sporting Club committee had invited me as their dinner guest and the chief contest was to have been a final eliminator for the British lightweight championship between George Feeney and Ricky Beaumont. Five days earlier Beaumont had cried off with an injury and matchmaker Les Roberts had a problem. Then he remembered his old friend Ken Buchanan, once world, European and British lightweight champion, who recently had reluctantly agreed to retire following pressure from the BBBC and close friends. Why not offer the thirty-seven-year-old craggy Scot one final performance of only eight rounds in the club where he had made his professional debut seventeen years earlier and where he had won the British title three years later? It would give Ken a small bonus and a chance to stage a dignified farewell.

One of the finest boxers Scotland had produced had fallen on hard times and his face was that of an old warrior who had lost his exceptional speed and timing and whose defence was now too easily penetrated. Only a couple of months earlier we had watched him as a substitute facing one Lance Williams at Wembley on a night when there were more empty seats than customers. It was not pleasant viewing for those of us who remembered Ken's outstanding talent when he had waged many fierce wars in hostile territory. The old Buchanan would have won easily, but the youth and greater strength of Williams earned him the decision and left the Scot's face bruised and cut.

Why did Ken persist against advice to destroy a legend? His

reason was a cliché in boxing: he was broke. The champion, who had once owned a Rolls-Royce, a small hotel and other property in Edinburgh, had declared when retiring in 1975 as undefeated European champion that he and his family would never be in want. But the Scot was forced to make a comeback four years later on his thirty-fourth birthday. For more than two years he struggled, doing it all from memory, and won four of eight contests. His marriage had also broken down. After losing to Williams, he agreed to have only one more fight, in Lagos, Nigeria. He had been offered £5000 and badly needed the cash. It looked as though it would be a painful pay day for Buchanan, but the contract never arrived from Nigeria, so he was glad to accept the chance to fight at the NSC.

It was an emotional occasion. Ken, of course, showed flashes of his class but this was not sufficient to keep Feeney away. Happily a sparkling eight rounds of science and goodwill followed and members had to be reminded of the club rules to cheer only at the end of each round. Ken was as gracious in defeat as he had once been arrogant in victory. After congratulating Feeney, he grabbed the mike and announced his farewell, thanking the club for its long support and Les Roberts, who had been with him for his first and last fight. Members stood and cheered and into the ring came the nobbins in the form of some screwed-up £1 notes and silver coins. Nobbins are usually tossed into the ring by a crowd delighted by the efforts of two poorly paid novices or six-rounders who have fought themselves to a standstill. The former world champion, who had grossed some £200,000, was neither too embarrassed nor too proud to share a mere £30 with Feeney. One of Britain's most skilled champions left the ring for the last time with dignity and, to the sound of cheering, made his way to the small dressing room to dab his slightly bruised face and pocket his £15 bonus.

The ultimate sadness was that this great champion, who had rashly retired more than once unnecessarily, now wanted to fight on in his twilight. A year later Buchanan climbed into a ring to take part in an unlicensed contest against an unknown opponent for a small payment. Ken won, but realized at last that the final bell had tolled.

Journey's End

On a damp and cold day in November 1980 they brought Johnny Owen home to Merthyr from Los Angeles. Thousands lined the high street as the large coffin of American oak carried the thin body of the brave little champion on his last journey from the old iron town to Pand Cemetery at the foot of the frosty peaks of the Brecon Beacons. Forty-five days earlier, in sunny California, Johnny, so phenomenally thin for a fighter that he was affectionately known as the Matchstick Man, had been knocked unconscious after twelve brave rounds in a bid to take the WBC bantamweight championship from the muscular Mexican Lupe Pintor. He never regained consciousness. After two brain operations to remove blood clots a life-support machine kept him alive but he remained in a coma as his mother and father, Edith and Dick, kept a bedside vigil.

Johnny Owen was only twenty-four. Though he stood 5 ft 8 in tall, he weighed only 8 st 6 lb and carried so little flesh that his ribs protruded. Some Merthyr fans had presented him with a cardboard skeleton which he regarded as a mascot and had it carried into the ring before a fight. He was the puniest-looking pugilist since Jimmy Wilde, from Quaker's Yard, Tylorstown. Wilde was so thin he was almost a freak, yet he was the most devastating flyweight the world has known, knocking out bantam and sometimes featherweights. Owen's thin frame brought gasps from ringsiders who watched him for the first time. But, like Wilde, his appearance belied his strength and stamina, which he had built up with five-to-ten-mile early-morning runs over the mountains and frequent fifteen-round sparring sessions in a local gym at night. Johnny Owen was not a natural fighter like Howard Winstone, who also came from Merthyr, but he worked at boxing from being a seven-year-old to become a distinguished champion. He lost but eighteen of 124 amateur contests and but one of twenty-seven as a professional before facing Pintor. He won the British Commonwealth and European titles. His only defeat for the European title against Juan Francisco Rodriguez in Spain was sheer robbery, but he took the title from the Spaniard in a return meeting at Ebbw Vale. In all those contests he had never been knocked out or knocked down. His jaw must have been durable. Sadly, no one knew until after he died that his skull was abnormally thin.

Apart from his painful thinness, he was almost unique as successful fighters go. He was quiet and shy and it is remarkable that he never seriously dated a girl. He was a lovely, good natured young man who adored his family. He had four brothers and three sisters. He opened a food store and had hoped, with the extra £10,000 purse he was to receive from the Pintor fight, to buy a pub or small hotel which all the family could share. Even though a triple champion, he remained the perfect son, and in the family home on the Gellideg council estate at Merthyr where he lived with his parents and younger brothers and sisters he still volunteered to light the fires and wash up.

Apart from his mother, who was naturally concerned whenever he appeared in the ring, the Owen family never had any fears for Johnny. It was usually his opponents who needed sympathy when the Matchstick Man went into action. He had put up a formidable and courageous exhibition in the Olympic Auditorium at Los Angeles. Local scribes and Mexican fans almost ridiculed his skeletal appearance and so dubbed him the Bionic Bantam or Oliver Twist, but they were astonished at his stamina, aggression and courage against the robust Pintor. Johnny was ahead after eight rounds but lacked the punch to rock the Mexican. Pintor began to get on top by the ninth round when he put the Welshman down for a count of three. From then on Pintor took over as the Mexican crowd screamed for blood. Only courage kept Johnny going as he was severely punished. Then the fatal round 12. A short right dropped

Owen for four. He rose and stood for the mandatory eight count but was a beaten fighter. The Mexican knew it and calmly placed a ferocious right which poleaxed the Welshman and the back of his head hit the floor with a sickening thud. Poor Johnny Owen would never wake again.

Back home in Merthyr they prayed for a miracle but miracles are few and far between and when forty-five days later the coffin was borne in that valley of tears and heroes which has witnessed so many tragedies this century, strong men like Eddie Thomas, a former champion, who became a manager and promoter, and Dai Gardiner, who managed Johnny, and many fight fans with deep emotion questioned the validity of professional boxing. But it had been Johnny Owen's choice. He loved boxing. It was the only profession he knew and was good at. He lived for the sport and, alas, died for it.

Speed is dangerous and more lethal than professional boxing. If a young man is killed in a motorcycle accident, it is pointless to say with hindsight that he should never have driven fast, particularly if he loved to speed. Lupe Pintor was hooked on speed. Three years after the Mexican had knocked out Owen and defended the bantam title a total of ten times, just failing to win the super bantam title from Wilfred Gomez, he was involved in a near fatal motorcycle accident which left him with multiple fractures. After an operation and six months' convalescence, he spent a further period in traction at his home at Cuajimalpa believing he would never fight again. The Mexicans prayed for Lupe Pintor and in 1984 he surprised his doctors by coming back to win two fights. But in July of that year he announced on television that he would never box again. Yet in August 1985, at the age of thirty, he amazed the medical men and the boxing scribes by winning the WBC junior featherweight title, beating Juan Kid Meza in Mexico City. This success was short-lived. A few months later in Bangkok Pintor was flattened in five rounds by Samart Payakaroon of Thailand, and quit for good.

The Mugging of a Legend

It happened in the so-called Swinging Sixties. The paunchy little man in the bowler hat was alone one night as he approached Cardiff station on his way home. A bunch of teenage thugs attacked him, an old man, who had already past his span of three score and ten years. They mugged him and their cowardice achieved what only one other man had done to this long-retired boxing champion in more than eight hundred fights. They knocked out Jimmy Wilde, the world's most renowned little fighter. The only other time the fabulous Jimmy Wilde was counted out was in the very last contest of his long career when Pancho Villa took his world title in seven rounds in New York. Jimmy was then thirty-one and had been out of the ring for two years, but he has been tempted by a £13,000 purse – astonishing money for a flyweight in 1923. In that fight Wilde was badly concussed and taken to hospital.

Jimmy Wilde was not a well man at the time he was mugged. A car accident ten years earlier had slowed him down and he had become diabetic. But the shameful attack was to end his active days completely and he spent the twilight of his life at Whitchurch Hospital, Cardiff, well cared for by the nurses and staff and vaguely happy, though he was never quite aware of what was going on even when they kindly made him a cake for his seventy-fifth birthday. He did not even know that his wife Elizabeth, a school-days sweetheart whom he had married at seventeen and who used to spar with him wearing a homemade breastplate, had died. Jimmy himself left this world peacefully a couple of months before his seventy-seventh birthday in 1969.

He had taken part in more than 150 recorded contests but claimed to have had 864 punch-ups after leaving the South Wales mines as a boy to box in Jack Scarrott's booth. On a busy day he would take on perhaps twenty all-comers for a few shillings. He was the first official world flyweight champion; though the limit was 8 stone, he weighed closer to 7 stone and had even boxed at 6 st 10 lb. Yet he took on top-class opponents well above 8 stone and on occasions up to 9 stone.

I never saw him fight but I first met him soon after his retirement when he was a frequent visitor to my father's house. Though a child, I grew to admire the man with the twinkling eyes and impish smile. I was amazed that this gentleman, known as the Mighty Atom and the Ghost with the Hammer in his Hand, had been the terror of world flyweights. As a soldier he had once fought for a purse of diamonds instead of cash. When he fought Pete Herman, one of America's best bantam champions, he had to concede the best part of 12 lb. Herman refused to weigh in at the scheduled time so Wilde declined to fight, but because the Prince of Wales (later to become the Duke of Windsor) was at the ringside he agreed to go ahead. He took a hammering but refused to stay down and eventually in the seventeenth round the referee, Jack Smith, picked him up and dragged him to his corner, saying, 'Jimmy, I just had to rescue you because you don't know how to quit.' He still did not know how to quit when KO-ed by those thugs.

BOOK FIVE

THE ECSTASY

Something Special

The handsome Adonis from Louisville, Kentucky, who, though still a teenager, advertised himself in huge letters embroidered on the back of his silk dressing gown as 'Cassius Clay – the Greatest', was more than a super-heavyweight like Johnson, Dempsey, Louis or Marciano. His combination of unusual talent and extraordinary personality made him something special. He rescued boxing in America from the hangover of the fifties and the financial stigma of the first Patterson–Johannson title clash.

After winning the Olympic light-heavyweight gold medal as a scraggy 6 ft 3 in eighteen-year-old in Rome in 1960, Clay turned professional. He revolutionized the sport in the United States, introducing ballet, grace and a sweet science, and also brought theatre, burlesque and a general sense of fun never known before in such a physical business. His individuality and his sense of rhythm had never been seen in boxing before, and with the aid of television he captured billions of new followers throughout the world, including millions of women who for the first time regularly watched a champion in action. He made the title a real world championship, defending it or giving exhibitions in all the big American cities and in London, Paisley, Toronto, Gothenburg, Frankfurt, Caracas, San Juan, Port of Spain, Buenos Aires, Zurich, Tokyo, Vancouver, Dublin, Jakarta, Kinshasa, Kuala Lumpur, Manila, Munich and Nassau. He was a true champion of the world, the people's champion, more famous and recognizable than any king, queen, president, film or pop star. His like had not been seen before and I doubt if it ever will again.

One of the reasons for the big slump in America had been the sport's gross over-exposure on television. Greedy promoters and managers were grabbing the cash and fight fans were staying at home or watching the fights in bars. By the sixties the Friday nights at Madison Square Garden, which once had regular 18,000 sellouts, had dwindled to 1000 fans, with no more atmosphere or life than a mausoleum. With Sonny Liston twice flattening Patterson in world title fights, American boxing was even more downgraded.

The smiling Olympic champion, with a syndicate of wealthy Louisville businessmen behind him, was a wholesome sight compared with Liston. Angelo Dundee was hired to train and advise him and between 1960 and 1962 Clay won all his ten professional bouts, mostly inside the distance. His style and speed belonged to the arts rather than the ring. Dundee brought him from Kentucky to Chicago during the first Patterson–Liston championship. He stole the show, to the annoyance of the PR boys hired by the Chicago promoters. He was all smiles, claiming that he was not only the Greatest but also the Prettiest! In Los Angeles he had been matched with a great old fighter Archie Moore, who had been hired a couple of years earlier to teach the lanky Kentucky kid a few tricks. Cassius, as immature as an Irish gossoon, was friendly and wide-eyed when Angelo Dundee told him to recite his homemade rhymes; Cassius obliged in parrot-like fashion:

'When you come to fight
Don't block the aisle and don't block the door.
I'll say it again, I've said it before,
Archie Moore will fall in four.'

'Little Sir Ego' was my summing up of this twenty-year-old, but he laughed and was so much more relaxing to be with than the gruesome Liston or the tense Patterson. And, sure enough, Archie Moore fell in four.

Clay was then matched at Madison Square Garden against Doug Jones and for the first time in twenty years the Garden was completely sold out. He won on points, and Jack Solomons brought him to Wembley three months later to meet British heavyweight champion, Henry Cooper. Like Jack Johnson and Sugar Ray Robinson, he stopped the traffic in Piccadilly and

needed a police escort as he held up his right hand and declared:
'This ain't no jive,
Cooper will fall in five.'

Though the young prophet proved to be right again, he had not bargained for Henry catching him with the famed left hook at the end of the fourth round. Only Dundee's astuteness saved the Kentucky colt from what could have been his only knock-out defeat. Clay had cut Henry pretty badly and was clowning a little towards the end of the round, probably intent on fulfilling his boast that Cooper would fall in five. But what a shock for Clay as he backed on to the ropes: Henry's left hook landed smack on his unprotected jaw and down he went, his eyes spinning. If only Cooper's punch had landed a fraction earlier! The bell had saved Clay from defeat, but he recovered quickly and with Henry still bleeding as he came out for round 5, the American's left jab was like a scalpel as blood gushed from Cooper's cuts and the referee called a halt.

Clay's next date was with Sonny Liston for the world title at Miami and the brash Kentuckian was declaring:
'Liston is great
But he'll fall in eight.'

I cannot recall a fight with more bizarre scenes before, during and afterwards. Weeks before the contest Clay conducted a psychological war, going into Liston's territory looking for the 'big, ugly bear'. His performance at the weigh-in six hours before battle commenced was more like the Mad Hatter's party. Long before Liston had stripped, Clay and Budini Brown, his cornerman and jester, came into the room screaming, 'Where's the big, ugly bear?' and 'Float like a butterfly, sting like a bee! Rumble young man!' To add to the noisy confusion, Budini was banging on the floor with what looked like a huge pogo stick. Cassius made mock attempts to get to Liston while Budini put on an act of restraining him. The general reaction was that Clay was a little crazy. Liston sat there stone-faced, not showing the slightest emotion. He raised one finger of his right hand to us all, indicating that was how long he thought the fight would last. Clay had worked himself into a state of excitement. Dr Alexander Robbins of Miami Beach Boxing Commission told us that his blood pressure was way up and his pulse almost double its normal rate. A little indiscreetly the doctor added,

'Clay is reacting as if he is scared to death of Liston.'

In the afternoon I took a swim and met Bud Schulberg. 'Have you heard the rumour that the fight's off?' Bud asked. I dashed off to check and a Miami reporter added to the confusion with 'Clay's flipped his lid. He's gone to hospital.' After a chase round town the rumours proved false. I arrived at the Convention hall early in the evening and met Angelo Dundee. He chuckled at all the rumours and slipped me into Clay's dressing room. Cassius was sitting completely relaxed in his white robe, his eyes almost closed.

When both boxers faced each other in the ring before the first bell, Liston tried his intimidating stare, but Clay outstared him. And then we were entertained to the most graceful exhibition by any heavyweight ever. Cassius moved like a ballet star, avoiding Liston's lunges with only the slightest turn of his head as he stuck a left jab into the champion's face. Liston had twice demoralized Patterson with his menacing tactics. Now he himself was bothered and bemused by a youngster who would not be bullied. The monster was suddenly impotent and pathetic as a swelling appeared under his left eye. He fumbled.

Yet there was a crisis midway through the fifth round. Apparently some liniment had passed from Liston's gloves into Clay's eyes. He stopped dancing and almost stopped boxing, backing away and rubbing his eyes. There was a doubt that he would finish the round. As the bell went Dundee soaked Clay's face with a sponge, but the boxer protested that he could not see and could not continue. Angelo shouted at him, 'You're winning. Go out and take the title!' He pushed him into the ring. Liston had witnessed the commotion and came out for round 6 swinging both fists. Clay began cautiously by back-pedalling but later stabbed Liston with two heavy jabs and the champion realized his chance of saving his title had gone. He slumped on his stool declining to come out for round 7, complaining he had damaged his shoulder. It was a shameful capitulation and the crowd began booing and chanting: 'Fix! Fix! Fix!'

I was assisting Eamonn Andrews with the inter-round summaries for the BBC. Eamonn had climbed into the ring to talk to Clay as pandemonium broke out throughout the hall. Eamonn could not get back for fifteen minutes, so I had the task of telling Britain in the early hours of the morning what was going on.

There are still some who believe that this contest and the disastrous return were fixed. So many rumours persisted that I wrote a column asking 'Hi Diddle Diddle, Was It a Fiddle?' But I do not believe either fight was fixed. I believe that Liston, like all bullies, had a yellow streak, and I am convinced that Clay never took part in a shady contest.

The return fight was scheduled for Boston. Clay, now heavyweight champion, revealed that he had joined the Black Muslims and insisted on being addressed as Muhammad Ali. Sordid rumours about the first fight caused some local politicians to try to prevent the fight taking place in Boston, and when it was forcibly postponed because of an emergency hernia operation on Ali it was moved to Lewiston, Maine. Only one serious right-hand punch was thrown, and though some said they did not see it, I certainly did. It was a good right to Liston's jaw. He went down and stayed down. It was all over in less than two minutes. I believe Liston was hurt, but I would not say he could not have got up; but then I did not rate him as one of the bravest of fighters.

Ali continued to grab the headlines. It was the time of the Vietnam war. As a Muslim, Ali refused to join the army and was heavily criticized, but he defended his title eight times, including a second win over Henry Cooper in six rounds in London in 1966. The following year he was given a five-year jail sentence for refusing to become a soldier. He did not go to prison but his passport was taken away and eventually every boxing commission declined to recognize him as champion. He announced his retirement and did not fight for three years. But public opinion on Vietnam changed. His sentence was dropped and he returned to the ring in 1970, stopping Jerry Quarry and Oscar Bonavena before taking on Joe Frazier who had won the title in Ali's absence. They met at Madison Square Garden in 1971 and what a great contest!

Ali had changed his style after his enforced absence. He no longer floated like a butterfly. Instead of avoiding blows with his amazing defensive skill, he seemed set on proving he could take punishment. In the first round he allowed Frazier to hit him many times on the chin, turning his head to the crowd to indicate he was not hurt. It was a punishing fight and very close. Ali had a lump on the side of his face the size of a small orange and Frazier was badly cut and bruised. Joe had put him down in the last round and Ali did well to get up but the knockdown cost him the decision. I do not believe Frazier would have beaten Ali but for his long absence; Muhammad twice defeated Joe later in New York and in a brutal title brawl in Manila.

It was a pity that Ali was no longer the ballet star. He was to prove himself the bravest of fighters, but he took unnecessary punishment and was to have his jaw broken by Ken Norton. He allowed many crude fighters like Leon Spinks to hit him at will and take his title when he did not appear to be in top condition, though he proved a point when he beat Spinks to win the heavyweight crown for a record third time. His ego forced him to attempt another comeback in 1980 when he faced Larry Holmes in a bid to become champion a fourth time. He had nothing left and retired after ten rounds, the only time he failed to finish. And he had still one more fight, against Trevor Berbick at Nassau in 1981, when he was a few weeks short of forty. Berbick held the Canadian and Commonwealth titles but was never in the class of the real Ali. Yet he easily outpointed the shell of the Greatest in his last appearance. In twenty-one years as a professional, Ali had lost only five of sixty-one bouts.

For me Ali's greatest performance was when he regained the title from George Foreman at Kinshasa, Zaïre, in 1974 when he was thirty-three. Foreman, Olympic heavyweight champion in Mexico, had developed a Liston monster image by blitzing Frazier in two rounds in Jamaica, Norton in two rounds in Caracas and a non-runner, Jose Roman, in one in Tokyo. Each fighter was to collect $5 million which had been put up by President Mobutu's government.

Foreman began a strong favourite but received a bad cut to his eye in training and the fight was postponed a month. Zaire insisted that as the purse money had been paid neither fighter could leave the country. This suited Ali, already a hero in Africa. But the delay did not suit the introverted Foreman. He had brought his mascot, a massive sheepdog, to Zaire, and the animal had to go into quarantine. The unhappy champion found himself in quarters surrounded by barbed wire and soldiers with tommy guns. Ali had spacious quarters at N'Sele near Mobutu's residence. So far as Zaire was concerned, Ali was the champion and thousands of children followed him for miles when he did his daily roadwork. This took place at 4 a.m. to coincide with the time of the fight, which was scheduled to suit American television. Ali began a psychological war against Foreman, referring to him as the 'Big Belgian' – before independence Zaire had been the Belgian Congo. He boxed fifteen rounds in training against Larry Holmes and other sparring partners, declaring, 'I'm gonna dance all night and the Big Belgian won't ever catch up with me.' But dancing was the last thing he intended doing.

Before the fight began Ali and Dundee were in the ring examining the ropes and Angelo helped to slacken them as Ali tested them with his own weight; that is something that would not have been allowed in America or Europe. Foreman was far from relaxed when the fight started but came out swinging. Ali did not get up on his toes dancing. He grabbed the champion and turned him backwards onto the ropes. Without realizing it, Foreman was already the victim of what Ali called his 'rope-a-dope' tactics. A little aimlessly the champion punched away at Ali's body as Ali grabbed, pulled and generally outmanoeuvred him. When Foreman could not land his big punches with which he had dismissed Frazier and Norton, he was just another big boy lost. Ali jabbed, outboxed him and continually belittled him with jibes, destroying his morale. Foreman was ready to be taken when he came out for round 8. His confident challenger wasted no time and began putting over right crosses. One put Foreman down. He was physically and mentally exhausted and quite confused. He did not get up. Ali was champion again. Poor Foreman was never the same fighter: he never regained his self-confidence and two years later quit boxing to become a preacher.

I have one last memory of Ali's sense of fun. A few American and British writers were invited to President Mobutu's palace. The President was waiting when the heavyweight champion arrived. Without regard to protocol Ali said, 'Mr President, I've been a citizen of the United States of America for thirty-three years and was never invited to the White House. It sure gives me pleasure to be invited to the Black House!' The President of Zaire had a different sense of humour. He did not even smile.

Whether Ali would have beaten Dempsey, Louis or

Marciano remains a matter of opinion. All of them at their peak beat the best around. But there is no doubt that between 1960 and 1980 his extraordinary personality changed the face of world boxing. He was indeed something special.

Henry the One and Only

Henry Cooper was not as great as the man he fought against twice, once as Cassius Clay and again as Muhammad Ali, but in his own way he is just as unique and something special in the world of boxing. Cooper is a phenomenon in the sense that, in any sport, with few exceptions, most champions once dethroned, quickly join the long queue of yesterday's men. Boxing is probably the hardest-hit of all. A cricketer or footballer slows down and slips gradually. A track man or tennis player can be beaten in one match and go on to win another, but if your boxing hero loses, it can be the end of his career and he is often physically demolished and perhaps rendered unconscious into the bargain. A fickle public remembers a champion was only as good as his last fight. Not so with Henry Cooper. Like some wines, he seems to improve with age when it comes to popularity and he received as big an ovation in 1984 on his fiftieth birthday as he did between 1954 and 1971 when he was fighting. In fact, he has become more popular than Ali, who came to London for Henry's birthday party but has not been able to maintain the fantastic adulation he received when ruling the world of boxing.

What is the magic behind 'Our 'En-ery' as he was, and still is, called by fight fans? Is it the memory of the famed left hook ('En-ery's 'Ammer'), which put out so many opponents and came within an ace of inflicting what would have been Ali's only knockout defeat? Was it the emotional sympathy of the public who protested against the decision in 1971 in favour of Joe Bugner which relieved Cooper of the European British and Commonwealth titles as he approached his thirty-seventh birthday? Perhaps it is due to the disappointing performances of the nine successors to Henry's old throne? How many of the following heavyweight champions since Cooper could you have named: Jack Bodell, Danny McAlinden, Bunny Johnson, Richard Dunn, John L. Gardner, Gordon Ferris, Neville Meade, David Pearce, Hughroy Currie, Horace Notice?

Compared with them, Cooper became a legend during his professional career of nearly seventeen years. He held the British championship for almost twelve years, longer than any other heavyweight champion, defending it successively nine times and regaining it from Bodell after giving it up in protest in 1969. He is the first and only British boxer to win outright three Lonsdale Belts. His record speaks for itself and explains his long honeymoon with the boxing public, but this alone cannot account for his continual popularity. There is no mystique. He just happens to be one of the sport's nice guys who has not changed or been the slightest bit spoilt since, as a Cockney kid, he took up boxing along with George, his twin brother, at Bellingham Boxing Club.

Henry Cooper's service to British boxing has been remarkable and so far has spanned over thirty years. He brought charm and emotional excitement into the toughest sport in the world, and through the medium of television his natural and unassuming honesty gathered hundreds of thousands of boxing supporters who had never been to a boxing match in their lives. Mums and old ladies and hundreds of kids simply adored him and adopted him as 'Our 'En-ery'.

Cooper will be the first to endorse the statement that he owes a great deal to his manager, the late Jim Wicks, a tough Cockney character who guided him during his tender years. It was, in fact, the fractured speech of old Jim, whom Henry found himself imitating without realizing it, that helped increase his fans on television. Brother George never developed the patter of Wicks.

Wicks was born in Bermondsey where they used to produce champions. His father was a docker, but Jim first became a street bookie and was later accepted to Tattersall's before turning to managing fighters. To Wicks a gymnasium was a 'jimmy-nasium' and a good guy was a 'luv-erly geezer'. If he could not recall the name of an old fighter it was either 'Charlie Wotsisname' or 'Bill Wodicallim'. Jim invented 'En-ery's 'Ammer' and talked about an opponent as a 'nice boy'. His schooling was brief but the Jim Wicks lexicon was an education in itself. And Henry was a quick learner.

Cooper's success did not come to him quickly. In the army George was reckoned to have the brighter future as a boxer and was a pretty good puncher with his right until he broke his thumb. Henry had a tremendous left jab and with this as his best punch he won an ABA light-heavyweight title. He relied on his jab after turning professional in 1954. It was not until 1958 that we saw Henry's left hook developing into the most lethal punch in British boxing. It was almost as though he discovered it the first time he fought Dick Richardson, at Porthcawl. Henry had gone through a bad time in 1957, losing three successive title fights – against Joe Bygraves (Commonwealth), Ingemar Johansson (European) and Joe Erskine (British). He seemed finished as a top-liner, but after re-establishing himself with three bouts in Germany he took on Richardson. The Welshman almost had him beaten in five rounds. Cooper's left eye was gashed when a right sent him toppling. As he rose, Richardson rushed in for the kill but a short left hook sent Dick crashing down and out! Jim Wicks introduced 'En-ery's 'Ammer' into the boxing dictionary.

After this, Henry again climbed off the deck to beat the rated American Zora Folley, then thrashed Brian London to become British champion in 1959 and the country's best-loved boxer. It is an amazing achievement considering that his long slender left hand had been fractured four times and that his left elbow, damaged in an accident at fourteen, had once been described by doctors as like an elbow belonging to a man of seventy! Also it is remarkable that he overcame the tremendous handicap of suffering from badly cut eyes in his early days. In his two fights against Ali Henry's face was a mask of blood from the cuts around his eyes and he underwent several operations for the removal of scar tissue. After the second Ali bout in 1966 he won three European and three British title contests.

Henry Cooper will always be remembered for putting Clay on the seat of his pants at Wembley in 1963. Only four seconds of round 4 remained when the young Cassius, not yet world champion, was clowning on the ropes. Cooper, bleeding from a deep gash above his left eye, was deadly serious and let the 'Ammer go. Clay's eyes spun round as he sank to the canvas. He struggled up at four, then unfortunately for Cooper, the bell sounded the end of the round and Angelo Dundee came to Clay's rescue. Running along the apron of the ring, he steered his dazed protégé back to the corner where Clay flopped on to the stool. Dundee slapped Cassius hard on the face, produced smelling salts and squeezed cold water from a sponge over his head. Clay was still dazed and Dundee used his trump card. He protested to referee Tommy Little that Clay's glove was split and appealed to the stewards at the ringside for new gloves. This request was not granted but Dundee secured an extra 30-second interval for his bemused fighter, and 90 seconds' rest makes Tunney's 14 seconds long count a trivial stay of execution. Whenever I joke with Dundee about the incident and ask whether he cut the glove his eyes twinkle. We must leave it as one of boxing's unanswered questions, but without Dundee in his corner at Wembley, Cassius could have faced a knockout defeat.

Clay and Cooper met again for the title in 1966 at Arsenal football ground. Clay, now Ali, did not intend to be caught by the left hook and again cut Henry's brow. The fight had to be stopped in the sixth round.

Henry remained an active British hero for another five years. In March 1971, when beginning to slide, he narrowly lost his three titles on a controversial decision to Bugner. Though a little bitter about the verdict, he conducted himself in public, as always, with great dignity. In his dressing room he turned to a crowd of us and said softly, 'Well, gentlemen, this is it. I have fought my last fight.'

It was a wise decision. He had become even more popular as a loser than as a long-time winner. Only two other fighters, Dempsey and Louis, grew in popularity after retirement in the way that Cooper did. Ali, the most acclaimed boxer the world has known, stayed around too long for his own good and lost to Larry Holmes and Trevor Berbick, which robbed him of some of the titanic adulation and respect that he enjoyed when he was the Greatest.

The Henry Cooper era brought joy and pride to British boxing. He remains an ambassador in retirement. He is also something special.

Warrior of Peace

No pugilist in the history of world boxing has been in the position of Barry McGuigan, the most talented and most loved boxer to come out of Ireland. He is not only the best champion the Green Isle has produced but probably the best British featherweight since peerless Jim Driscoll, despite his ill-fated trip to Las Vegas where under the desert heat he lost his WBA title to a substituted opponent, Steve Cruz, from Texas.

McGuigan is equipped with a devastating left hook and a competent jab and right cross; he is a commendable survivor. He is both a warrior and a pacifist and in a troubled land is accepted as an ambassador of goodwill by Northern Ireland and the twenty-six counties of the Republic. There can be few public places in Belfast where thousands of Protestants and Catholics can gather under one roof and be completely united. Whenever Barry McGuigan fights at the King's Hall there is a temporary truce. Religion and politics are put aside as Irishmen unite to watch him in the ring. That night they are one nation. There is no north and south. McGuigan is Irish and so is every proud supporter.

Attending the King's Hall whenever a son of Ireland is defending or challenging against a foreign invader is a traumatic experience. In the days long past when Billy Spider Kelly, Rinty Monaghan, John Kelly, Jim Warnock, Bunty Doran, Freddie Gilroy, John Caldwell and other splendid Irish champions were in action, I could feel the great tension getting to me as in no other arena. The chauvinistic roar of Ulster fight fans can sound frighteningly hostile to a stranger. It seems to rise to a crescendo and bounce off the roof. It is a tribal war cry and must be intimidating to the visiting gladiator.

Never has the King's Hall been so united as one roaring voice than since the arrival of McGuigan. Though he had to go to London to bid for the WBA title from the masterful Eusebio Pedroza because of the huge financial demands made by the man from Panama to risk his title in Britain, he kept his promise to defend it for the first time in Belfast. This was against Bernard Taylor, from Tennessee, and with Taylor demanding an extra £75,000 to fight in Belfast and the police restricting the attendance at the King's Hall to 6000, McGuigan's share of the gate was considerably smaller than if the fight had taken place in America or London. To give some idea of the influence that this featherweight with the hands of a heavyweight wields not only in Ireland but throughout the world, 18 million viewers watched him win the title from Pedroza on BBC television, compared with nearly 16 million regular fans of 'Coronation Street' on ITV. Among those sending congratulations were President Ronald Reagan and Dr Garret Fitzgerald, the Irish Prime Minister, who personally telephoned to say, 'You are making an enormous contribution to the cause of reconciliation in Ireland.' A party to end all parties was taking place at Clones, 100 miles over the Ulster border, where McGuigan's parents live. When he went to Dublin two days later it was estimated that 100,000 people jammed O'Connell Street as Barry received their adulation from the top of an open bus.

McGuigan, slightly built, with a thin moustache and pale skin, is an unlikely looking pugilist, the sort a bully might pick on to his cost. A teetotaller and a non-smoker, he represents all the good things about boxing and about a great nation whose heart has been pierced by religious and political bitterness and which has seen cruelty and murder carried out on the streets by a minority of violent men from both sides. McGuigan was born a Catholic at Clones, Co. Monaghan, but married Sandra, a Protestant girl. He moved and became a UK subject in order to box for the British title. For this he received threats from the IRA. It has not frightened him away. His mission outside the ring is to do everything he can to unite his divided countrymen.

He achieved this when he tamed the skilled Taylor, who claimed he had won 489 of 498 amateur contests and was undefeated in thirty-four as a professional. Taylor boxed beautifully for six rounds and was ahead, but he wilted when McGuigan began sinking a left hook into his body and, after walking wearily to his corner after eight rounds, informed his manager he could not continue.

Then suddenly there seemed to be too much pressure put on the little Irishman. With his bookmaking manager Barney Eastwood he planned a million dollar future by taking his title to America. Was he now fighting too often?

The first evidence of fallibility of Ireland's new hero was revealed in his next fight, the defence of the WBA title in Dublin. He was due to face the Argentinian champion, Fernando Sosa, but the South American was not fit and Barry faced a little known substitute, Danilo Cabrera, from the Dominican Rupublic. It looked an easy touch for the Irishman, but Cabrera gave him unexpected trouble and cut his eyes before McGuigan finally stopped him in the fourteenth round.

But the plans were on for the Irishman to join the new millionaires of sport, and he agreed to defend the title against Sosa in New York or Las Vegas. Vegas turned out to be the most lucrative venue and this was the biggest mistake the McGuigan camp had so far made. To suit US television, which provides the bulk of boxing cash, McGuigan accepted to enter the ring in the heat of the afternoon. Las Vegas heat in June has to be sampled to be believed.

It was discovered that the Argentinian had to undergo eye surgery and so Barry was to face another substitute challenger, Steve Cruz, a tall boxer and a favourite with the Vegas fans. It should have been easier for McGuigan, who was made the 9-1 favourite, but something went seriously wrong. Barry just was not the same fighter who had the experts declaring him to be a greater featherweight than Nel Tarleton or Howard Winstone.

The first big shock came when he had trouble making the weight. He had to go on the scales three times. In the tremendous heat he should have had no difficulty in making nine stone. Barry fought well early in the fight as he had done against Danilo Cabrera, yet he was getting caught too easily and wasn't slowing down Cruz with his famous left hook. With the temperature at 110 degrees and much higher inside the ring under the television lights, McGuigan began to visibly wilt and after a magnificent battle the second shock came when Cruz, after being under heavy fire, dropped the Irishman with a stinging left hook. Barry was hurt and waited on one knee for a count of nine.

To McGuigan's credit, despite showing distress, he fought back like a true champion. He was cut above the eyes and Cruz became confident, as it was obvious to every onlooker that he was now able to hurt the champion more than Barry had been able to hurt him. McGuigan had built up a good lead but could he last out fifteen rounds? He threw a careless low left hook in the twelfth round and had a vital point deducted. Yet he could still have kept his title if he could stand up, but his strength had been sapped by the heat and by Cruz's power, and he was dropped twice in the final round. He managed to survive but was completely exhausted with the final bell sounded and a unanimous decision went to Cruz.

McGuigan was taken to hospital. He was dehydrated and two brain scans were ordered. Thank heavens he had no damage but, like Cooney and Bruno after their shattering defeats by Holmes and Witherspoon, suffered terrible depression. He even considered quitting for good.

With hindsight, the McGuigan camp made a horrendous mistake going to Las Vegas. It wasn't worth the hassle and the abnormal heat for all the money in the world. New York would have been a better venue. As champion he could have insisted on fighting in London or Belfast once more. Things just weren't right in Las Vegas. The set-back diminished him as a superstar in America but he remains a hero in Ireland and Britain and it was not, I believe, the real McGuigan who failed in Las Vegas.

Barry is a wealthy young man and I wouldn't urge him to stay around the ring too long. Whatever he decides about his future, he has done a super job for his country as the warrior of peace.

TV's Golden Boy

Many of the problems that started in the sixties, such as violence and promiscuity, are blamed on television. But two guys who will assure you that television is the greatest invention since Cinderella's fairy godmother are George and Billy Walker, former Billingsgate fishporters from London's East End. Thanks to television, Billy, the kid brother, became a golden boy overnight at the age of twenty-one and, without winning a professional title, grossed £250,000 in thirty-one contests, which brother George, also a former boxer, turned into £500,000 by shrewd business investments. Billy retired at thirty to join the tax exiles in Jersey. George as managing director of Brent Walker, the highly successful leisure group, became a millionaire.

For George it was a case of gloves being sweeter the second time around. Ten years older than Billy, he won an ABA light-heavyweight title in 1951 and turned professional the next day. He, too, never won a professional championship, but he showed himself to be a brave fighter in a losing battle for the British title against Dennis Powell at Liverpool Stadium in 1953. With his left eye completely closed and blood gushing from various cuts, he battled on for eleven rounds before his corner retired him. His fee was only £800 and much less after deductions. Three fights later he retired, at twenty-four. His career of fifteen bouts had grossed around £5000. With the help of a loan from his father-in-law, he raised a mortgage to buy a garage for £15,000.

Billy was a schoolboy at that time. He helped in the garage

and later worked at Billingsgate. He had grown bigger than George and weighed around 15 stone, but he preferred swimming to boxing and only joined the West Ham Amateur Boxing Club at eighteen to get fit. George persuaded him to try on the gloves and was delighted to discover that he could bang a bit. Billy entered and won the ABA heavyweight title in 1961 at the age of twenty-one.

Although professional boxing was seldom seen live on television in the sixties, the ABA had a contract with BBC for their championships and internationals. As the new amateur heavyweight champion Billy was picked for Great Britain against the United States and 12 million viewers were glued to the little box hardly believing their eyes as Britain led the match 9–0. The last contest of the international was between the heavyweights and the good-looking blond East Ender stepped in against Cornel Perry, a 17-stone black American. One minute 55 seconds later Perry lay like a warrior taking his rest. Britain for the first time ever had whitewashed America 10–0. Next morning the name of Billy Walker was on everybody's lips. He was prematurely being hailed as Britain's new 'White Hope'. A few months later another 12 million watched him flatten Emil Svaricek, the Austrian heavyweight champion. By now a dozen fight managers were chasing to sign him up.

Brother George had his own ideas. He realized that Billy, as a good-looking heavyweight, would be bigger at the box office than he had been. He intended to take over as sole manager. It was just a question of when Billy would turn professional – before or after the Commonwealth Games which were to take place in Australia? I took George aside at the 1962 Boxing Writers' Club dinner and asked him for the answer. George said he had not made up his mind, but a few days later he walked into my office with Billy to say he was signing for three fights with Harry Levene for £9000. With the BBC fees that sum increased to £13,500. The brothers would go into a business partnership on a 50–50 basis including the garage.

Billy was an immediate box-office success and for seven years, win or lose, Wembley was always sold out. He set a Wembley record. He had the men roaring and the women screaming as he bravely bulldozed forward, collecting millions more supporters on television. He was, understandably, given a build-up against a few mediocre Continentals, and the fact he was held to a draw by Spain's Mariano Echevarria in his second fight was proof he had a great deal to learn. One or two fighters were imported, who were not worth their air fare, and Billy duly put them away. Still the 'House Full' sign went up every time he appeared. Two of his best battles were against Johnny Prescott, the Birmingham heavyweight in 1963. Billy won the first on a stoppage in the last round and lost on points in a closely fought punch-up six months later.

The money poured in from promoters and television. George became a little over-optimistic. Billy was such an attraction that attempts were made to build him up for a possible meeting with Ali and a huge purse, but defeats by Brian London, then a veteran, and Eduardo Corletti put paid to this ambition, despite more knockout wins against moderate opposition.

Billy had two title fights. The German Karl Mildenberger stopped him in eight rounds for the European crown and Henry Cooper cut him up in six rounds for the British and Commonwealth championships. In each case Billy was out of his depth but fought with characteristic courage. He gave all he had in both encounters.

It was after Billy was stopped by Jack Bodell in eight rounds in 1969 that the Walkers decided enough was enough. Billy was only thirty but it was clear he would never now win a title. The brothers had grossed a quarter of a million pounds from fights and doubled it with business investments – the garage and a chain of eating houses called Billy's Baked Potato.

The worst that could be said about Billy Walker is that he never learned about the finer arts of fighting and his defence did not improve after seven years. His early promise of being a devastating puncher was not fulfilled, but he always had a go and possessed more than his fair share of guts. He sometimes left the ring cut and badly bruised but would walk into my office four days later, his face almost back to normal. George claimed they had some remarkable cream for taking out bruises. The golden boy lost eight of thirty-one professional fights, but he always gave the crowd value for money, ignoring defence and going to war.

When he quit the ring Billy also ended the partnership with George, who was going from strength to strength financially.

They did a deal and Billy, an autograph hunters' target, went back into anonymity, retreating to Jersey. I once met him in London and had to look two or three times to make sure it was Billy Walker. He had dyed his blond hair black to avoid being recognized. He owns property in the Channel Isles and has a guaranteed income for the rest of his days. When I asked why he had not remained in business with George, he explained, 'I hate the hassle that George loves and I like money but not to gamble with. George will borrow millions from the bank to build up his empire. That would frighten me to death.' George's empire of Brent Walker is still growing. He controls golf courses, squash courts, banqueting suites and many restaurants. He has produced and distributed a number of successful films with stars such as Joan Collins and Albert Finney. He also has put Gilbert and Sullivan operas on video at a cost of more than £2 million.

The Walker Saga is one of boxing's success stories. The two sons of a brewery drayman from London's East End loved boxing without being quite good enough to win professional titles. Yet where would they be today without boxing? Still at Billingsgate Market?

The Tycoon

On 8 February 1965 a press conference was called at the Hilton Hotel in London's Park Lane on behalf of Terry Downes. The boxing writers went along expecting to be given the final details of Terry's return fight with Willie Pastrano for the world light-heavyweight championship. Instead we were in for the unexpected. Downes, with an air of solemnity that was out of character, announced he was retiring. He was only twenty-eight. He could not resist a couple of wisecracks as he continued, 'I was ready to have another go at Pastrano but Willie wanted the lot. I didn't mind buying my own programme last time, but if I fight him again I'll have to pay for my own ticket.' The Pastrano camp were demanding £30,000. This would have left Terry with around £4000. He might as well have been an amateur by the time he had paid his sparring partner, his manager and his tax bill.

Terry estimated he had grossed around £150,000 in the ring. After tax and expenses, he had managed to keep about half of it but, as British fighters went in the fifties and sixties, Terry was unique. He was already a tycoon, owning a Rolls-Royce and a luxury house at Mill Hill which had cost £6000; nearly all his cash had been put into trust for his wife and children. Though he had held the world and British middleweight titles and had come close to beating Pastrano for the light-heavyweight crown, Terry's tycoon status was little to do with throwing punches. It came from betting shops.

It was mainly due to some smart thinking by Jarvis Astaire, who realized that a fortune could be made when betting shops became legal in England. The Hurst Park Syndicate was formed and Terry and his astute manager Sam Burns became executives and were each able to turn £2000 into £200,000. It had all begun modestly enough with Terry transforming the premises of a small secondhand car business into a betting shop. In a comparatively short time Hurst Park Syndicate had twenty-five betting shops, was valued at £1 million and was still growing. Better things were to come. The William Hill Organization eventually took over, with Burns becoming managing director. Later Charlie Clore took over William Hill. It was good news that Terry Downes, ex-world and British champion, could retire a rich man, unlike so many champions. Two months earlier he had thrilled 6000 fans at Belle Vue, Manchester, when, after ten rounds, it seemed the British fighter might cause an upset by grabbing Pastrano's light-heavy crown. The American had cuts around both eyes and, after an early lead, seemed to be fading but, unfortunately for Britain, after a bullying from Angelo Dundee, Willie came out in round 11 and like a tremendous professional desperately gambled all with a right hand that put Terry down. The Londoner hauled himself up with an effort, but was chastized before going down again. Courage brought Downes to his feet once more at six, but he was hurt, and Andy Smyth, one of the super-referees, stopped what would have been a hopeless cause. It was a shame for Terry. If he had not been careless in round 11 he might have won the world 12 st 7 lb crown, and Downes naturally would have liked to finish at the top.

Terry had been a real professional. He had lost more blood than any donor, standing up to some real beatings early on, the heaviest against the American Spider Webb, but, always his own man, he had in-bred courage and survived to hold the world title for a short spell. He was not the most talented middleweight Britain produced but there was not one with more guts. Born at Paddington in West London, fate took him to America as a sixteen-year-old. His sister Sylvia, a trapeze artist, lost an arm in a bus accident in the States and her mother and father rushed across the Atlantic to see her, taking young Terry with them. He loved America and stayed on, joining the US Marines and winning many boxing honours with them. He returned to England and joined the famous Fisher amateur club in Bermondsey before turning professional and fighting for Jack Solomons in the days before Sam Burns switched his boxing loyalties and linked up with Jarvis Astaire, Harry Levene and Mickey Duff.

Downes kicked off with Solomons to a sensational build-up but was stopped by Dick Tiger, an outstanding Nigerian middleweight, who did most of his early fighting in Liverpool. Terry was also outpointed by Les Allen and was prematurely written off. But in 1958 he collected the vacant British title, beating Welshman Phil Edwards. Nineteen fifty-nine was a bad year. Downes was badly cut up by Spider Webb, stopped with cuts by Michael Diouf and after flooring Cowboy McCormack ten times was disqualified for a low punch and lost his title.

The gutsy Cockney regained the title by stopping McCormack six weeks later and in 1960 won a Lonsdale Belt outright when he stopped Phil Edwards in twelve rounds. Then followed what I rate as one of his best performances, a points win over Joey Giardello at Wembley. He took part in a series of three fights for the world championship against Paul Pender, losing twice in Boston and winning once in London. He later beat Americans Don Fullmer, Sugar Ray Robinson and Phil Moyer in London. Robinson was forty-five at the time and Terry is too honest ever to expect to be put in the same league as a Robinson ten or twenty years younger.

Downes was stripped of his British middleweight title for declining to accept a purse offer from Jack Solomons to defend the crown. Downes maintained the offer was peanuts. This was at the time when Solomons was feuding with Astaire, Duff, Burns and Levene. Downes decided to box as a light-heavyweight, won three ordinary contests and was given a crack at Pastrano. He did his best and failed, but he wisely did not press his luck by making the plea of so many old champions – 'just one more for the road'.

Terry was lucky. The Betting Act helped make him a tycoon at twenty-eight and that is a far happier story to relate than that of so many champions who finished broke.

THE LAST ROUND

I have attempted to deal fairly with the good, the bad and even the ugly of world boxing, and also the agony and the ecstasy that come as the result of failure or success. I have not attempted to minimize the risks – everyone should be quite clear about the danger when ducking under the ropes – but I oppose those doctors and politicians who want the sport made illegal. I prefer to leave the individual the right to choose. For many outstanding champions boxing has been an escape from poverty and unbelievable squalor, especially in the Deep South of America, in the ghettos of big cities and in the Third World. I have spoken with champions who admitted that they would have been delinquents heading for crime if boxing had not given them the opportunity to develop their only talent. Unfortunately, because of the riches a good fighter can pull in, boxing attracts unscrupulous characters who exploit young boxers without a head for figures, just as the new wealth in sports like tennis, golf, soccer and snooker will attract some agents who are no more than opportunists. There are good and bad in all walks of life, and this sort of situation will never be completely eliminated unless human nature itself changes.

All has not been perfect in the past and much is still not perfect today. What of the future? We must learn from our mistakes. There has been a tremendous drive to make the sport safer. It can never be injury-free and there will always be the occasional fatality. But with the increasing number of medical checks fighters are now being protected from unnecessary risks. Licences have been withdrawn after brain scans or optical examinations revealed weaknesses or defects. The World Boxing Council, formed in 1964, is by no means perfect, but it has brought about some improvements in the sport. It has a membership of more than a hundred nations and has spent much time on safety, introducing medical examinations and drug tests and insisting that a doctor is at ringside in countries where such precautions used to be disregarded. The WBC insurance scheme provided nearly $100,000 to meet hospital expenses for poor Johnny Owen and in 1985 the Council donated another $100,000 to further research into safety. More and more efforts are being made in Britain, which has led the way in safety, despite the fact that some boxers, encouraged by their managers, resist attempts to prevent them from continuing to box even though they have been informed that it is not in the best interests of their health for them to carry on. They are fools to themselves and if allowed to go on fighting they may pay for their disregard in a tragic manner.

Inevitably, politics plays a tremendous part in world boxing. There are three governing bodies – the World Boxing Council operates from Mexico, the World Boxing Association from Panama and the International Boxing Federation from New Jersey. The British Boxing Board of Control is affiliated to the WBC and the WBA and to the European Boxing Union. The WBA's strength lies with its Latin American and South African members and promoter Bob Arum, with the blessing of the WBA, has staged world title fights in South Africa. In contrast, the WBC does not deal with South Africa. The IBF is pro-American and, when formed, the Federation introduced a rule allowing only an American citizen to become its president.

The problem with having three world bodies is that, with the number of weight divisions increased from eight to fifteen or sixteen by each organization, it is possible to have nearly fifty world champions, instead of eight, as in the old days when five out of ten men in the street could name most world and British champions. The WBC claim they introduced seven new in-between weights to make boxing safer. In some parts of the Third World there are champions at super flyweight, flyweight and junior flyweight. Light-heavyweight and cruiserweight were once the same, with a limit of 175 lb; this meant that a fighter of, say, 177 lb might have to face a heavyweight or any weight. This seemed unfair, so now all three bodies accept light-heavyweights up to 175 lb. The WBC have put a 195 lb limit on light-heavyweights. The IBF, Britain and the Commonwealth go along with this, but the WBA call this division junior heavyweight, restricted to 190 lb! The IBF have introduced super middleweights, bringing their number of divisions to sixteen. In Britain we now recognize twelve different weights.

Personally I consider it a nonsense to have a situation which produces so many world champions. I defy even the expert to name the current world champions without a record book to hand. However, the situation suits the promoters, the television interests and the commissions because it means they can have more world championship fights, as they do regularly in the gambling hotels of Las Vegas and Atlantic City. But familiarity breeds contempt and world titles have been cheapened. Any boxer with a fair record and the right connections has a chance of getting a crack at the world title, and he probably will not mind which version – WBC, WBA or IBF – he fights for provided the cash is right. We have so many superweights and junior weights that it is no longer an outstanding achievement to win two world titles at different weights. Even winning three titles is not as remarkable as when Henry Armstrong achieved this feat. In recent years Wilfredo Benitez, Alexis Arguello and Roberto Duran all held world crowns at three weights, including a junior weight. It will not be long before some fighter becomes the first to win four titles.

It used to be considered an achievement to become the heavyweight champion of the world. From the days of John L. Sullivan down to Muhammad Ali, there were few men around who could not name the heavyweight king. Joe Louis reigned supreme for a record eleven years nine months. Since Ali retired the heavyweight championship has had three claimants at a time. Ali must wince and Louis turn in his grave at some of the strangers in paradise – John Tate, Mike Weaver, Michael Dokes, Gerrie Coetzee, Greg Page, Tim Witherspoon, Pinklon Thomas, Tony Tubbs, Trevor Berbick and Michael Spinks.

Don King, who stages many regular heavyweight title fights, talked sense when he ridiculed the situation of having three heavyweight champions all reigning at the same time. He declared that he would stage tournaments to eliminate two of them so as to end up with one undisputed heavyweight champ. King was, as usual, talking through his pocket. We will never get back to the days when a world champion was strictly the best boxer at that weight. I personally regret this a great deal. Boxing needs television as much as television needs boxing, but we must not allow television to present boxing as mere entertainment rather than as a sport, in the way that it does wrestling. There was a scandal in America a few years ago when Don King planned regular tournaments for ABC under the title 'US Boxing Championships'. Accusations of rigged records and ratings caused the television company to pull out. It would have turned out to have been a highly suspect venture had it gone ahead, but ABC had been willing to sink $1.5 million in the project at the start. Fortunately, incidents like this are few and far between. Nevertheless, ruling bodies must be alert for anything, no matter how small, that could bring the sport into disrepute.

At least we know there are few irregularities, such as rigging, in Britain. In the days before control the promoter was the boss and some of them made doubtful decisions. As a boy I was at the Greenwich Baths in southeast London one evening to see the local heavyweight, Jack Stanley, fight Don Shortland, a big Yorkshire contender. Shortland must have won the first seven rounds, but in the last round Stanley put him down three times. The crowd was roaring for the local fighter. The referee, a former British champion, clearly indicated to the promoter, who was acting as MC, that Shortland was the winner, but the promoter announced the decision as a draw. The crowd was delighted and the referee kept quiet. That sort of thing does not, and could not, happen today.

Boxing, well controlled, well promoted and properly supervised, is a tremendous and exciting sport. I travelled many thousands of miles covering fights in North and South America and in most countries in Europe and I enjoyed every trip, even those that ended in disappointment for the British boxer. After travelling to Buenos Aires when Dai Dower was knocked out in the first round by Pascual Perez and to Chicago for a postponed meeting between Marciano and Walcott, with the rearranged fight also ending in the first round, a well-known New York columnist gave me the title of 'One-Round Butler'. That is how I was known when I used to go into the once famous Toots Short's bar and restaurant. It was hard to shed the name after I returned to the States for a one-round repeat by Liston over Patterson in Las Vegas, and yet another one-rounder at Lewistone, Maine, when Ali put Liston away in their second meeting. I have watched many thrilling encounters involving Ali, Frazier, Archie Moore, Sugar Ray Robinson and dozens of others, great fighters all. It is the uncertainty that makes the fight game exciting.

There used to be more characters in boxing, both in America and Britain, than in any other sport I have covered, and though some survived because they never broke the Eleventh Commandment by getting found out, they were colourful guys, the kind who inspired Damon Runyon to switch from being a boxing reporter to become one of the most successful of short-story writers. As a schoolboy I shook Runyon's hand when he visited London with Dempsey. I did not meet him again until 1946. My father and I joined him for a sad dinner in New York. Runyon had cancer and his larynx had been removed. He communicated with us with the help of a pencil and pad. He scribbled, as we expected, that Dempsey was the greatest and that boxing was still his favourite sport. I shook hands knowing I would never see him again. His ashes were scattered from a plane over his beloved Manhattan.

I met many super-champions who were also ambassadors of the sport outside the ring, men like Dempsey, Tunney, Louis, Marciano and Ali, and I made friends of Britain's heavyweights, like Jack Petersen, Tommy Farr, Len Harvey, Larry Gains, Don Cockell, Henry Cooper and many more. The doctors, politicians and do-gooders who want to see boxing banned would do well to consider the philosophy of Tommy Farr, who began fighting in the booths when he was twelve and after more than a hundred tough contests was still fighting at nearly forty. Shortly before he died on St David's Day, 1986, I asked Tommy a question concerning his epic fifteen-round stand against Louis for the world title nearly fifty years earlier. He laughed and said, 'Do you mind? Every time I hear the name Joe Louis my nose starts to bleed!' Then he added, 'But if we could put the clock back I would fight Joe all over again.' To evoke such a response, boxing must be, surely, civilized conflict.

Index

Adams, Ida, 153
Agramonte, Omelio, 20
Ali, Muhammad (Cassius Clay), 1, 17, 27, 32, 43, 44, 45, 91, 92, 101, 102, 103, 106, 107, 109, 116, 126–9, 155, 160, 165, 179–86, 187, 189–90, 205
Allen, Les, 201
Allen, Terry, 136
Amateur Boxing Association (ABA), 3
Ambers, Lou, 22, 23
American Medical Association (AMA), 3
Anderson, Jimmy, 81, 167–8
Andrews, Eamonn, 182
Angleman, Valentine, 57
Angott, Sammy, 13
Antuofermo, Vito, 35, 36, 70, 131–2
Arcel, Ray, 39, 54, 112, 155
Arguello, Alexis, 46–7, 139, 205
Armstrong, Henry, 10, 15, 21–4, 120, 122, 152–3, 157, 205
Arum, Bob, 2, 91, 92, 107, 126–9, 133, 204
Association of Boxing Commissioners, 6
Astaire, Jarvis, 84, 95–6, 200, 202
August, Bernd, 102
Australian Medical Association, 3

Baer, Buddy, 20
Baer, Max, 10, 18, 66, 67, 69, 70, 90, 106, 157–8
Baksi, Joe, 77, 105–6, 119, 147
Barrett, Mike, 84, 95, 96, 132, 134–5
Barrow, Lily, 17
Barrow, Munroe, 17
Barton, Albert, 74
Basilio, Carmen, 15
Beale, Pee Wee, 13
Beaumont, Ricky, 170
Becket, Arnold, 140–1
Beckett, Joe, 9, 65, 95
Bell, Frank, 69
Benaim, Gilbert, 94
Benitez, Wilfredo, 32, 40–1, 205
Berbick, Trevor, 184, 190, 205
Berg, Jack Kid, 5, 10, 53–6, 123
Berlenbach, Paul, 90
Berrocol, Carlos, 130
Beshore, Freddie, 20
Best, Johnny, 93
Bidwell, Doug, 130
Bird, Bill, 123
Bivins, Jimmy, 20
Blin, Jurgin, 101
Bodell, Jack, 101, 102, 188, 198
Bonavena, Oscar, 183
Boon, Eric, 10, 93, 141
Botham, Ian, 140
Braddock, Jim, 18–19, 69, 70, 90, 106, 158
Bramble, Livingston, 140
Brewer, Honey, 13
Brion, Cesar, 20
British Boxing Board of Control (BBBC), 3–4, 11, 54, 95, 99,

Index

BBBC – *contd.*
119, 133, 138, 204
British Medical Association
(BMA), 1, 3–4
Britton, Jack, 123
Broadribb, Ted, 66, 67, 75–6, 77, 124
Brooks, Pat, 17
Brown, Budini, 181
Brown, Freddie, 155
Brown, Jackie, 10, 57–8
Brown, Jimmy, 136
Brown, Joe, 10
Brown, Panama Al, 10
Brown, Phil, 100, 101
Bruno, Frank, 103, 135, 159
Buchanan, Ken, 10, 40, 70, 83–6, 170–1
Buchanan, Tom, 83
Bugner, Joe, 92, 96, 101–3, 188, 190
Buonvino, Gino, 29
Burman, Red, 69
Burns, Sam, 94, 95, 96, 201, 202
Burns, Sid, 94
Buxton, Alex, 148
Bygraves, Joe, 189

Cabrera, Danilo, 194
Cabrera, Norberto, 36
Caldwell, John, 10, 136, 192
Callahan, Mushy, 53, 54–5
Capone, Al, 115, 118
Campbell, Jim, 57
Candel, Carmelo, 62
Canzoneri, Tony, 53, 54
Cappell, Jack, 94
Carbo, Frankie, 5, 91, 115–18
Carey, Tom, 89
Carnera, Primo, 18, 90, 93, 99, 120, 158
Carpentier, Georges, 9, 45, 61, 65, 89–90, 93
Carstens, Dave, 66
Casey, Jack, 62
Cerdan, Marcel, 10, 11, 38
Chaplin, George, 100
Charles, Ezzard, 20, 30, 119, 120, 121

Charnley, Dave, 10
Chocolate, Kid, 53, 55
Christie, Errol, 37, 134–5
Churchill, Jobey, 66
Clark, June, 13
Classen, Willie, 122, 124
Clay, Cassius *see* Ali, Muhammad
Clore, Charles, 201
Cochran, Charles B., 93
Cockell, Don, 10, 11, 30, 106, 157
Coetzee, Gerrie, 103, 204
Coffroth, James J., 89
Colombo, Al, 28–9
Conn, Billy, 10, 19–20, 45, 90, 121
Conrad, Harold, 161
Conteh, John, 10, 139
Cooney, Gerry, 44, 100–1
Cooper, George, 188, 189
Cooper, Henry, 10, 92, 99, 101, 123, 124, 131, 180–1, 183, 187–91, 198
Corbett, 89
Corinthians, 92–3
Corletti, Eduardo, 198
Corro, Hugo, 36
Costello, Billy, 47, 50
Cowdell, Pat, 134
Crawford, Frankie, 82
Cronin, John, 111–12
Crowley, Dave, 93
Cruz, Steve, 194
Cullen, Maurice, 84
Cummings, Jumbo, 103
Currie, Hughroy, 188
Curry, Bruce, 49–50
Curry, Don, 11, 48–50, 107, 134
Cuthbert, Johnny, 124

Daly, Bill, 84, 116, 118–19, 124, 128
Daly, Nipper Pat, 124
D'Amato, Cus, 91, 99
Damski, Paul, 119
Danahar, Arthur, 157
Daniels, Adele, 148
Daniels, Frankie, 27
Daniels, Gipsy, 74–5
Davis, Sammy Junior, 160

Day, Doris, 160
Dempsey, Jack, 1, 5, 9–10, 17, 19, 26, 69, 89–90, 118, 190, 207
Diamond, Legs, 115
Dickson, Jeff, 54, 62, 66, 93
Dimes, Albert, 110, 112
Dingley, George, 59
Diouf, Michael, 202
Dokes, Michael, 205
Doran, Bunty, 136, 192
Dower, Dai, 206
Downes, Sylvia, 201
Downes, Terry, 15, 96, 109–12, 200–1
Doyle, Jimmy, 4
Driscoll, Jim, 11, 78, 168
Duff, Mickey, 84, 95, 96, 132, 202
Dundee, Angelo, 32, 33, 44, 155, 180, 181, 182, 185, 190, 201
Dundee, Johnny, 123
Dundee, Vince, 62
Dunn, Richard, 102, 155, 188
Duran, Roberto, 32–3, 37, 39–42, 83, 85, 108, 154–6, 205
Durelle, Yvon, 27

Eastwood, Barney, 194
Echevarria, Mariano, 198
Ecklund, Anders, 103
Edwards, Phil, 202
Eleta, Carlos, 39, 41
Elvin, Arthur, 58, 63, 93, 119
Epperson, Lee, 28
Erskine, Joe, 189
European Boxing Union, 3, 204
Evangelista, Alfredo, 44

Famechon, Johnny, 82
Farr, Tommy, 5, 10, 19, 65–9, 70, 75, 123, 157, 158, 207
Feeney, George, 170, 171
Ferris, Gordon, 188
Finch, Albert, 72, 73
Finnegan, Kevin, 35, 131–2
Fitzgerald, Garret, 193
Fitzgerald, Ella, 160
Fitzsimmons, Bob, 61, 74, 104
Flowers, Bruce, 54

Folley, Zora, 189
Foord, Ben, 66, 157
Foreman, George, 2, 92, 107, 184–5
Foster, Bob, 45
Frazier, Joe, 43, 101, 103, 107, 183–4
Frazier, Marvis, 103
Fullmer, Don, 202
Fullmer, Gene, 15, 111

Gainford, George, 12–13, 15
Gains, Larry, 5, 63, 69
Galindez, Victor, 5
Gallouze, Farrid, 107
Gans, Joe, 90
Garcia, Ceferino, 23
Garcia, Jose Luis, 102
Gardiner, Dai, 174
Gardner, John L., 128, 188
Gavilan, Kid, 116
Giardello, Joey, 202
Gibbs, Garry, 72
Gibbs, Harry, 81
Gilroy, Freddie, 10, 136, 192
Gold, Sir Arthur, 140, 141
Goldman, Charlie, 29
Goldstein, Ruby, 14, 15, 21
Gomez, Wilfred, 174
Gould, Joe, 18
Graydon, Bill, 79
Graziano, Rocky, 2, 10, 11, 14, 37
Greb, Harry, 11, 123
Gregg, Eddie, 101
Green, Dave Boy, 105–6
Griffith, Emile, 4, 105

Hagler, Marvin, 1, 11, 31, 34, 35–8, 39, 41, 49, 130–3, 156
Haley, Leroy, 50
Hall, Dick, 101
Hampston, Len, 59
Hamsho, Mustafo, 37
Hansen, Jorgen, 106
Harding, Jack, 93, 94, 162
Hart, Mark, 73
Harvard, John, 3

Harvey, Len, 10, 61–4, 75, 93, 94, 123
Hawkins, Vince, 73
Hearns, Thomas, 33, 37, 39, 41
Heenan, John C., 2
Herman, Pete, 176
Hill, Charlie, 135
Hill, William, 96, 201
Hitler, Adolf, 19, 67
Ho, Andy, 145
Hogarth, William, 2
Holmes, Larry, 31, 43–5, 92, 100–1, 139, 165, 184, 185, 190
Hood, Jack, 10
Horrman, Kurt, 13
Howard, Arthur, 149
Howard, Kevin, 34
Hudson, Brian, 84
Hulls, Sydney, 66, 67, 93–4, 157
Hurley, Jack, 124
Hurst, Tom, 76

International Boxing Club (IBC), 91, 115–17
International Boxing Federation (IBF), 4, 139, 204–5

Jack, Beau, 120, 122–3
Jackson, Freddie, 140
Jackson, Melody, 22
Jacobs, Mike, 18, 19, 20, 67, 69, 90, 94, 165
James, Ronnie, 10, 117
Jeby, Ben, 62
Jefferson, Pat, 47
Jeffrey, Leroy, 79
Jofre, Eder, 82
Johansson, Ingmar, 99–100, 189
Johnson, Bunny, 102, 188
Johnson, Jack, 93
Johnston, Charlie, 26
Johnston, Jimmy, 26
Jolson, Al, 23
Jones, Colin, 48, 49, 134
Jones, Doug, 180
Jones, Leroy, 44
Jurich, Jackie, 60

Kalule, Ayub, 33
Kane, Peter, 10, 59–60, 157
Karoubi, Jimmy, 13
Kaylor, Mark, 37, 134–5
Kearns, Doc, 26, 118, 124
Kefauver, Senator, 117
Kelly, Billy Spider, 135, 136, 192
Kelly, Jim Spider, 136
Kelly, John, 136, 192
Kennedy, Robert, 117
Ketchel, Stanley, 11
King, Don, 44, 91, 92, 126–9, 205–6

La Motta, Jake, 10, 11, 12, 38
Lacey, Al, 109–10
Laguna, Ismael, 70, 84
Laing, Kirkland, 41
LaStarza, Roland, 11, 30
Lawless, Terry, 84, 103, 108
Leahy, Mick, 15
Ledoux, Scott, 44
Lee, Caveman, 37
Legra, Jose, 81, 168
Leonard, Juanita, 34
Leonard, Sugar Ray, 31–4, 36–7, 40, 48–9, 105–6, 154–6
Lesnevich, Gus, 70, 76, 107, 146, 157
Levene, Harry, 84, 94, 95, 202
Levinsky, Battling, 123
Levinsky, King, 18
Lewis, John Henry, 10, 45, 63, 72
Lewis, Ted Kid, 53, 84, 123
Liston, Danille, 160
Liston, Geraldine, 160
Liston, Sonny, 2, 91, 107, 109, 116, 118, 158–61, 180, 181–3
Little, Tommy, 190
London, Brian, 99, 103, 198
London, Jack, 75, 76, 94
Longstaff, Stanley, 94
Lonsdale, Lord, 54, 92–3
Lopez, Angel, 115, 116
Loughran, Tommy, 10, 45, 66
Louis, Joe, 1, 10, 12, 17–21, 29, 65, 67–9, 90, 100, 106, 116, 119, 120–1, 158, 160, 165–6, 190, 205

Lovaine, Lord, 2
Lovell, Alberto, 102
Luciano, Lucky, 115
Lynch, Benny, 10, 57–60, 162–4
Lynch, Bobby, 163

McAlinden, Danny, 102, 188
MacArthur, Douglas, 14
McAvoy, Jock, 10, 62, 63, 75, 94
McCarthy, Connie, 117
McCorkindale, Don, 145
McCormack, Cowboy, 202
McCory, Milton, 48, 49, 107
McGory, Johnny, 163
McGowan, Walter, 10
McGuigan, Barry, 4, 70, 107, 135, 168, 192–5
McGuigan, Sandra, 193
McKeown, Sam, 74
McNeely, Tom, 100
Madison Square Garden, 90
Mancini, Ray, 140
Mann, Nathan, 19
MAPS, 127–9
Marciano, Rocky, 10, 11, 18, 20–1, 27, 28–30, 35, 36, 43, 91, 107, 112, 116, 121, 206
Markson, Harry, 148
Marsden, George, 123
Marshall, Lloyd, 106, 107
Martin, Leotis, 160
Martin, Tommy, 75
Mason, Harry, 61
Matthews, Harry, 11, 29
Mauriello, Tami, 76
Maxim, Joey, 14–15, 26, 77, 106, 118, 147
Mead, Eddie, 23–4, 152
Meade, Neville, 188
Medina, Theo, 149
Meza, Juan Kid, 174
Middleton, George, 72
Mildenberger, Karl, 92, 198
Miller, Freddie, 10, 123
Miller, Johnny, 18
Miller, Ray, 15
Milligan, Tommy, 93
Mills, Charlie, 74

Mills, Chrissie, 145
Mills, Freddie, 10, 26, 61, 63, 70, 74, 94, 105–6, 107, 124, 145–7, 157
Minter, Alan, 10, 35, 36, 70, 130–3
Mitri, Tiberio, 148
Mizler, Harry, 55–6
Mobutu, President, 185
Monaghan, Rinty, 136–7, 149, 157, 192
Montana, Small, 58–9
Monzon, Carlos, 11, 38
Moore, Archie, 10, 25–7, 30, 45, 91, 99, 118, 180
Moore, Davey, 4, 41, 105, 155
Morgan, K. O., 162
Morton, Janks, 32
Moyer, Phil, 202
Mugabi, John, 38
Muldoon, John, 94

Napoles, Jose, 70, 108
Nash, Charlie, 85
National Sporting Club (NSC), 93, 170
Navarro, Ruben, 85
Nelson, Azumah, 135, 140, 154
Nelson, Battling, 90
Neusel, Walter, 11, 63, 67, 118–19
Norris, Jim, 90–1, 94, 115, 116, 117
Norton, Ken, 43–4, 107, 184
Notice, Horace, 188
Nova, Lou, 69

Obelmejias, Fulgencio, 37
Ocasio, Osvaldo, 44
Olin, Bob, 10, 66
Oliver, Shelton, 13
Olson, Bobo, 14, 15, 147–8
Olympic Games:
  1936, 67
  1960, 179
  1968, 140
  1972, 122
  1976, 31, 45
  1980, 48, 140
  1984, 4, 141

O'Sullivan, Danny, 136
Owen, Dick, 172
Owen, Edith, 172
Owen, Johnny, 4, 105, 172-4, 204

Paduano, Donato, 84-5
Page, Greg, 205
Palermo, Blinky, 5, 115, 116-18, 160
Palmer, Pat, 58
Palmerston, Lord, 2
Palomino, Carlos, 106
Paret, Benny, 4, 105
Pastrano, Willie, 200, 201, 202
Paterson, Helen, 149, 150-1
Paterson, Jackie, 136, 145, 149-51
Patterson, Floyd, 2, 27, 30, 91, 99-100, 107, 116, 159, 160, 180, 182
Payakaroon, Samart, 174
Pearce, David, 4, 123, 188
Pedroza, Eusebio, 70, 193
Pender, Paul, 15, 109-12, 202
Pep, Willie, 82
Perez, Pascual, 206
Perry, Cornel, 197
Petersen, Jack, 5, 10, 11, 62, 66, 94
Petrolle, Billy, 53, 54
Petronelli, Goody, 36, 132
Petronelli, Pat, 36, 130
Phillips, Eddie, 62, 63, 66
Pintor, Lupe, 4, 105, 172, 174
Pompey, Yolande, 27, 149
Powell, Dennis, 196
Powell, Ike, 109
Prescott, Johnny, 198
Price, Elliot, 109, 110, 112
Pryor, Aaron, 46, 47, 139
Puddu, Antoni, 85

Quarry, Jerry, 183
Queensberry Rules, 3

Radechmacher, Pete, 99
Ramos, Mando, 84
Ramos, Sugar, 4, 105
Reagan, Ronald, 193

Reddington, Tom, 75
Reid, Jesse, 50
Reynolds, Bernie, 29
Ribbentrop, Joachim von, 67
Richardson, Dick, 189
Rickard, Tex, 18, 89-90
Rinaldi, Giulio, 27
Robbins, Alexander, 181
Roberts, Les, 170, 171
Robinson, Edna Mae, 13
Robinson, Sugar Ray, 4, 10, 11, 12-16, 70, 71-2, 123, 149, 160, 202
Roderick, Ernie, 23-4, 141
Rodriguez, Juan Francisco, 173-4
Roldan, Juan Domingo, 37
Roman, Jose, 184
Rosenbloom, Maxie, 10, 123
Ross, Barney, 22, 23
Ross, Dr Oswald, 4
Routis, Andre, 53
Rudkin, Alan, 10
Runyon, Damon, 35
Russell, Sam, 136
Ryan, Sylvester, 116

Saddler, Sandy, 82
Saldivar, Vincente, 78, 80-1, 82, 167, 169
Sarron, Petey, 22, 23
Savold, Lee, 20, 29, 119
Sayers, Tom, 2-3
Scarff, Sam, 134
Scarrott, Jack, 176
Schmeling, Max, 5, 18, 19, 67, 75, 90
Schulberg, Bud, 99, 182
Scott, Phil, 65
Scypion, Wilfred, 37
Seales, Sugar Ray, 122, 124
Seki, Mitsunori, 81, 167
Servo, Marty, 13
Shapiro, Maxie, 13
Sharkey, Jack, 18, 90
Shavers, Earnie, 43, 44, 92, 103
Shibata, Kuniaki, 82
Shortland, Don, 206
Sibson, Tony, 37

Silverman, Sam, 109–11, 112
Sims, Robbie, 42
Simon, Abe, 20
Simons, Roger, 13
Sinatra, Frank, 165
Singer, Al, 55
Slade, Jim, 106
Smith, Evelyn, 13
Smith, Harold J., 126–9
Smith, Jack, 176
Smith, James Bonecrusher, 103
Smith, Lee, 127
Smyth, Andy, 201
Snead, Hurley, 140
Solomons, Jack, 13, 71, 76, 84, 93–5, 133, 157, 180, 202
Sosa, Fernando, 194
Spinks, Leon, 184
Spinks, Michael, 43, 44, 101, 205
Spinks, Terry, 79
Spot, Jack, 110
Stafford, Roger, 33
Stanley, Jack, 206
Steele, Eddie, 65–6
Stevens, Kirk, 141
Stock, Jean, 73
Stracey, John H., 10, 70, 108
Stribling, Young, 10, 93
Strickland, Maurice, 118
Strother, Shelby, 160
Suero, Jose, 41
Sullivan, 89
Suzuki, Ishimatsu, 85
Svaricek, Emil, 197

Tarleton, Nel, 10, 11, 78
Tate, John, 205
Taylor, Bernard, 193–4
Thil, Marcel, 10, 62
Thomas, Eddie, 79, 80, 81, 83, 84–5, 174
Thomas, Harry, 19
Thomas, Pinklon, 139, 205
Thompson, Billy, 95
Tiger, Dick, 202
Toma, Aurel, 162–3
Top Rank, 2
Torres, Jose, 5

Trainer, Mike, 32
Tubbs, Tony, 139, 205
Tunney, Gene, 5, 9–10, 28, 90, 107
Turner, Bob, 75
Turner, Jack, 74
Turpin, Annette, 147
Turpin, Carmen, 147
Turpin, Charmaine, 147
Turpin, Dick, 72, 73, 148
Turpin, Gwen, 148
Turpin, Gwyneth, 147
Turpin, Jackie, 72, 73
Turpin, Randolph, 10, 12, 13–14, 70–3, 106, 145, 147–9, 157
Tyson, Mike, 104

Usai, Giancarlo, 85

Valdes, Nino, 26–7
Valle, Victor, 44
Van Dam, Luc, 73
Vega, Louis the Bull, 32
Velasquez, Miguel, 84
Villasana, Marcos, 140

Wainwright, Steve, 36, 130
Walcott, Jersey Joe, 20, 29–30, 107, 119, 206
Walker, Billy, 103, 196–9
Walker, George, 196–9
Walker, Mickey, 11, 26, 93, 118
Wallace, Coley, 28
Wallace, Gordon, 148
Wallman, Hymie, 117
Walsh, Jimmy, 56
Warnock, Jim, 58, 59, 192
Warren, Frank, 96, 103
Waterman, Peter, 95
Watt, Jim, 10, 46, 83, 85, 108
Weaver, Mike, 44, 205
Webb, Spider, 201, 202
Weill, Al, 29, 91, 124
Wells, Bombadier Billy, 65, 93
Welsh, Freddy, 78
Wepner, Chuck, 160
Whalley, Tut, 57
Whiteson, Adrian, 4

Wicks, Jim, 94, 124, 188–9
Wickwar, Len, 123
Wilde, Elizabeth, 175
Wilde, Jim, 66, 75
Wilde, Jimmy, 66, 75, 78, 93, 136, 172, 175–6
Willard, Jess, 5, 19, 90
Williams, Ike, 10, 117
Williams, Johnny, 157
Williams, Lance, 170–1
Wills, Harry, 17
Wilson, Sammy, 58, 59, 163
Winstone, Benita, 79, 167
Winstone, Bronwen, 168
Winstone, Howard, 10, 11, 78–82, 167–9
Winstone, Roy, 167
Winstone, Wayne, 167
Wirtz, Arthur M., 116

Witherspoon, Tim, 134, 135, 139, 205
Wolf, David, 140
Womber, Bang Bang, 13
Woodcock, Bruce, 10, 20, 76, 94, 119, 131, 146–7, 157
World Boxing Association (WBA), 204–5
World Boxing Council (WBC), 3–4, 204–5
World Medical Association, 3

Young, Jimmy, 43

Zale, Tony, 10, 11, 37, 38
Zambrano, Manuel Esteban, 41
Zanon, Lorenzo, 44
Zivic, Fritzie, 13, 15, 24, 123